Street Outreach
Love, Service & Leadership

by Anthony Goulet

Foreword by

His Holiness The 14th Dalai Lama

For my mother Julie Goulet

The smaller we make ourselves, the more powerfully Spirit flows through us to serve others. And in serving others, we find everything we're looking for.

Foreword

I'm glad to know that Mr. Anthony Goulet's book, *Street Outreach: Love, Service & Leadership* deals with the problem of youths who are homeless, runaways and endangered. It is dismaying that the cries of those helpless and broken youths often go unheard. I am glad that there are initiatives like the Street Outreach Workers who provide much needed attention, affection and advice to those who have been through so much difficulty in life. I commend their compassionate action in bringing meaning to the lives of many youths who otherwise would have given up on life.

This book outlines the author's experience in the success of dealing with many youths who undergo traumatic experiences in life. I hope it will inspire other fellow brothers and sisters to do their bit to better the lives of the many young people who deep within yearn for our care and compassion.

~ His Holiness The 14th Dalai Lama

Prologue

My mother passed away during the writing of this book. She had been living with us for two years. It was an honor to care for her during the last part of her journey here on Earth. The reason I dedicate this book to her is because she is the one who the Creator used to set me on a path of service to others. Like many things in our lives, we see with great clarity in retrospect. Perhaps, we, as human beings should reflect more upon moments in our lives and take time to contemplate what happened, what's happening and prayerfully move forward. As it often happens, we get caught up rushing to meet deadlines and the conscious or subconscious pace of *busy* consumes us in its flow. The flow of busyness isn't of the Creator and balance. Busyness is a flow of worry and anxiety, leading to years gone by, where the blessed lessons are not picked up and carried, at least until something happens that rocks and stops our world.

Even when our world stops the rest of the world keeps on going, which used to frustrate me, but now I consider it a good thing. Let the world keep on going when your world stops. For the world will continue to do the same thing the world has always done – keeping its constant strain of seeking to fill voids only the Creator can fill. The world throws things, positions, titles and numbing agents at us, selling us on promises that someday, one day, perhaps with the next purchase, promotion or high, we will be all we can be. In the moments when our personal world is rocked, we see the truth of what matters, what no longer does and what never did. It's a gift. A gift we can carry and live or one we can ignore. The gift of what truly matters is what Street Outreach Workers carry and offer. That gift was given to me from the Creator through my mother in 1988.

A few months after my dad passed away in 1988 when I was sixteen years old, my mother asked me what I wanted to do with my life. I told her I wanted to make as much money as possible. After I answered her question, I asked her what she wanted to do with the rest of her life. She told me all she wanted to do was help people. When she said those words, I laughed and told her that was the stupidest thing I had ever heard. Months before she passed on I apologized to my mother for what I had said to her. She laughed and accepted my apology. I told her the irony of that moment was she awakened something deep within my soul. It took quite a few years and many mistakes for that awakening to manifest within me, but like all sacred seeds, eventually they took root and began to grow. I am thankful to the Creator, my mother and father, as well as the countless mentors and teachers the Creator has placed in my life who have helped me cultivate and grow within the sacredness I am, so I can see and serve the sacredness in others. Like my mother, I just want to help others in love and service. One way the Creator has called me to help others in love and service is as a Street Outreach Worker.

This book shares the works and miracles the Creator allows Street Outreach Workers to offer and experience. I am not speaking for, nor on behalf of all Street Outreach Workers, only myself, from my own experiences. The title of Street Outreach Worker is used throughout this book. A Street Outreach Worker may have the title of Violence Interrupter, Gang Interventionist, Violence Interventionist, Missionary, Preacher, Ceremonial Leader, Medicine Man, Medicine Woman, Pastor, Firefighter, Police Officer or Paramedic. What I have learned by living the calling of a Street Outreach Worker is regardless of titles, Street Outreach Workers strive to live more deeply within the humanity we are by serving the humanity within others. Street Outreach Workers explore and strive to manifest the fullness of love that all sentient beings are. Although I acknowledge the many variations of Street Outreach Workers aforementioned, this book is from my experience as a Street Outreach Worker serving homeless, runaway, endangered and trafficked youth and young adults, as well as my many years of work as a street-level Gang Interventionist. I have omitted names and other information in the stories I share in this book to protect the confidentiality of others. As with every book the Creator has written through me, this book has been read and approved by many of the youth and young adults I have been blessed to serve. Since some of them have given this book their stamp of approval, I am confident this book will bless you.

May this book bless you and guide you to reach deep within your heart to hear the Creator's loving voice, reminding you that you are a sacred blessing, miracle and gift, so you reach out to others and remind them of the same. May this book also, like that moment in time with my mother thirty years ago, be an awakening to the sacred, so no matter in what capacity you have been called to serve, you devote yourself completely to your sacred path of love, service and leadership.

In Love & Service,
Anthony F. Goulet

Sacred Callings

Street Outreach Workers

Some people go to work with a workbag that has a laptop computer, notebook, perhaps a day planner and their lunch. Other people go to work in a vehicle filled with tools necessary to construct or repair homes and businesses. First responders such as police officers, firefighters, EMS personnel, and military personnel go to work with lifesaving and life protecting equipment. Street Outreach Workers go to work with a carload of survival bags. Street Outreach Workers give the survival bags to fellow human beings who are struggling with homelessness. Each survival bag contains bottled water, nonperishable food such as MREs (Meals Ready to Eat), first aid kits, insect repellent, hygiene products, ponchos, blankets, gloves, socks, flashlights, cleansing wipes, and a note that reminds the person receiving the survival bag they are a sacred blessing, miracle and gift. The survival bags also contain a referral list of emergency numbers along with the business card of the Street Outreach Worker. Street Outreach Workers also carry another bag with them – a mental health first aid bag. The mental health first aid bag contains important tools that assist with engagement, connection and interventions. The mental health first aid bag contains a culturally competent mixture of items to meet someone where they are spiritually, mentally, physically and emotionally. My mental health first aid bag contains six

1

books, so if spirituality is important to the person I am serving, hopefully one of the books is from the spiritual path the person walks. The spiritual books I have in my bag are the Bible, Quran, Torah, Buddhist scriptures, Bhagavad Gita, and a book of Zen poems. Along with the books of Holy Scriptures from various religions, for those I am serving whose spiritual path happens to be Indigenous, my bag also contains a hand drum, Abalone shell, sage, cedar, sweetgrass, and a prayer feather. The mental health first aid bag I carry is stocked with writing journals, pens, pencils, crayons, markers, coloring books, a chess set, Uno playing cards, small poster boards to create life maps or vision boards, a few stuffed animals, and some essential oils for relaxation. It also contains some over-the-counter vitamins and amino acids to assist someone in getting through withdrawals, such as vitamins B, C, D and the amino acids Theanine, Acetl-L-Carnitine, and N-Acetyl-Cysteine (NAC), along with a supply of Gatorade, Imodium, Dramamine, Benadryl, Tylenol and Ibuprofen. The external tools a Street Outreach Worker uses are important, but it's within the sacred calling of a Street Outreach Worker, not the external tools, the lives of our most marginalized youth and young adults are healed.

Currently I have the professional title of Street Outreach Worker and Assistant Director of an Emergency Youth Shelter. Many people don't know Street Outreach Workers exist, and many who have heard of us, aren't familiar with what we do on a daily and nightly basis. Street Outreach Workers make up street outreach teams at various nonprofit organizations and ministries. The Creator delivers healing and restoration to others through us on the streets, in alleys, under bridges and inside drug houses. We are also vessels of the Creator's healing and restoration to the youth and families we serve from the crisis calls we receive from youth, young adults, parents, schools and law enforcement. We meet people where they are at, and we don't just meet basic needs such as food, water, clothing and blankets. We provide safe transportation to shelters and safe houses. We reunify families. We rescue people from human and labor trafficking. We facilitate suicide interventions. We also go into many different schools and communities and facilitate anger management, conflict resolution, peace building and prevention groups.

Is there any work more important than reaching out to our most marginalized and traumatized youth and young adults and delivering them to safety? Street Outreach Workers and those we serve understand the thin ice of symptoms society skates upon. People use many resources with endless meetings, policies and talk, but the dangers and causes lie deep below the thin ice of symptoms. The Creator calls Street Outreach Workers deep below the symptoms and takes us to the cause, which is a place few want to acknowledge exists, and even fewer are willing to go. Society has lulled itself into a sleepwalk more concerned with comfort and appearance than actual work. Where else is the real work to be done other than at the causal level? Maybe because Street Outreach Workers and those we serve have fallen below the thin ice of symptoms and into the abyss of freezing, isolating, dangerous causes, we know the importance of submerging ourselves where the work is not just needed, but the only place where it's effective. When people become as passionate, outspoken and supportive about ending human trafficking, homelessness, hunger and domestic violence as they are about money, political elections and professional sports, we will have Heaven on Earth. Until Heaven on Earth comes, Street Outreach Workers, although not the majority, are on call 24/7, on the streets day and night, going towards that which many people try to avoid. Any Street Outreach Worker will tell you, you don't have to go to another city, state or country to find youth and young adults who are homeless, hungry, hurting and trafficked, because it's happening right where you are.

Outreach is done everywhere, every day, in all our lives. Outreach is not only Street Outreach Workers responding to crisis calls in drug houses and under bridges. Outreach is a parent reaching out to their child, a child reaching out to their parent, or someone struggling with addiction reaching out to the Creator. We are all reaching out to the Creator and each other in an endless cycle of need. We are dependent upon the Creator and each other. There is no such thing as a self-made man or self-made woman. Just as a seed, no matter if it grows to become the mightiest oak tree in the forest, will never stop needing the Earth, we will never stop needing the Creator and each another.

Sacred Names, Sacred Titles

Anyone can have a title, and many do. Names and titles in and of themselves are not sacred. The sacredness of a name or title is determined by how a person carries it. A name or title does not make the person, the person makes the name or title. Street Outreach Worker *is* a sacred title. A sacred title, if treated as sacred, is understood as a calling, not a job. In the sacred calling of a Street Outreach Worker we grow within the calling of love, service and leadership by submitting to the will of the Creator of our personal understanding. Street Outreach Workers are lifelong students. In the sacred calling of a Street Outreach Worker we empty ourselves of ourselves, so the Creator can shine brightly through us to others.

Business Plan for Street Outreach Workers

Below are thirteen standard business plan question answered from the perspective of a Street Outreach Worker.

1. What are you selling? Nothing. The Creator, through the Street Outreach Worker, is giving away miracles. Street Outreach Workers hope the individual or family they are serving gets hooked. Not because at some point there will be a monetary payback, but because then the individual or family will know, not just believe, the Creator gives miracles for free. And those miracles are available twenty-four hours a day, seven days a week.

2. What problems are you solving? Sex trafficking, exploitation, homelessness, hunger, thirst, violence, substance abuse, alcoholism, hopelessness, depression, anxiety and trauma.

3. What is your mission and motivation? The mission of the Street Outreach Worker is to deliver love in the form of food, clothing, shelter, compassion and safety to every person we encounter. The motivation of the Street Outreach Worker is love.

4. What makes your business plan unique? Look around, my friend.

5. What is your destination? What will success look like for your business? Whether the Street Outreach Worker delivers miracles to one person or one hundred thousand people, the daily destination is cultivating Heaven on Earth. Success looks like a smile, a tear of joy and relief, a full belly, a thirst quenched, someone who was cold but is now warm, and someone who was in terror but is now secure in safety, laughter and freedom.

6. Who needs what you have to offer? Who is your ideal customer? The estimated over 300,000 victims of human trafficking in Texas. The estimated 4.5 million victims of sex trafficking worldwide. The estimated more than 2 million homeless children in the United States. The estimated 100 million people who are homeless throughout the world. The estimated 10 million men and women (twenty per minute) who are victims of domestic violence throughout the United States. The estimated 20 million children who live in a home without their father. The estimated 7.2 million abused children in the United States. All people throughout the world who are abused, hungry, homeless, traumatized, tortured, beaten and enslaved.

7. Who else could use your product or service? Anyone in need, whether their challenges are situational or chronic.

8. Why do people need your product or services? To be fed, clothed, housed, safe and to not be beaten, bought, sold or killed. To prevent abuse, hunger, homelessness, exploitation, murder, and to move those who have been traumatized to safety, stability, restoration, peace, post-traumatic growth and miracles.

9. Why should they buy it from you instead of one of your competitors? As already stated, there is no fee, miracles are free. In street outreach there is no competition, only cooperation. It matters not from where or who someone receives their miracle, only that they receive it. There can never be too many Street Outreach Workers.

10. Why will they return to you and refer others to your business? They may or may not return to the Street Outreach Workers, but we will return to them, every day and every night. Miracles are the referral source from the *Source*. There are no lack of referrals for Street Outreach Workers; it is an endless stream of human beings in need of miracles.

11. Why will you succeed, where other similar businesses have failed? Success is not the amount of people you serve, or the number of people who love your work. Success is love being your work. Whether the Street Outreach Worker succeeds in cultivating Heaven on Earth for one or one hundred thousand, success has occurred.

12. How will you market and promote your business? Street Outreach Worker's lives are the marketing and promotion, by bearing and delivering the fruits of connection, compassion and love under bridges, inside drug houses, abandoned buildings, juvenile detention facilities, domestic violence shelters, emergency shelters, or anywhere else the Creator calls us to meet the needs of others.

13. Where do you want your business to be five years from now? Nonexistent. The dream of the Street Outreach Worker is for human beings to awaken to our collective humanity and cultivate Heaven on Earth together, for everyone, all life, with no separation or lack, only the truth of love we are all created in.

Entry-Level

The calling of a Street Outreach Worker is not an entry-level position. It astounds me that some job postings for the position of Street Outreach Worker have the words *entry-level*. Street Outreach Workers have years of personal and professional experience, and most have their own powerful testimonies. Street Outreach Workers can and will go to places most people cannot or will not, to meet youth and young adults where they're at, while facilitating highly skilled interventions in uncontrolled environments; successfully reaching, then establishing relationships of trust with our most traumatized and marginalized youth and young adults. The calling of a Street Outreach Worker is not entry-level but is often the crucial point of entry for runaway, homeless, missing, and endangered youth and young adults to make their exodus from trauma and take their first steps towards healing.

Love is the Best Practice

You can research best practices in serving homeless, runaway and endangered youth, and you will find the critical role Street Outreach Workers have in serving our most marginalized youth and young adults. Any program will only rise to the level of those who are facilitating the program. A street outreach team does not require the stamp of approval from any institution. However, street outreach teams do require the stamp of approval from those they serve. There are efforts to professionalize street outreach and gang intervention by academia through degrees and certifications. Offering courses that provide degrees and certifications in such areas is not a bad thing. However, when academia states or implies that without their stamp of approval, programs that work no longer do or are questionable, then that is a bad thing because that is academic arrogance.

Street Outreach Workers have known about and worked with survivors of sex trafficking long before the term sex trafficking existed. Street Outreach Workers have known about and worked with youth and young adults to achieve post-traumatic growth long before the term post-traumatic growth existed. In the early 1990's we facilitated exercises with those we served to assist them in looking for the hidden strengths and gifts traumatic events bring us if we look for them. Academia has caught up to the truth that many grassroots programs, which spring forth in communities throughout the world, are best equipped to address and solve the challenges within their own respective communities. An excellent example of this is within Native American communities, where for centuries, the causes, effects and process of healing with historical and intergenerational trauma have been understood and implemented, long before academia began to talk about trauma-informed care.

Whether the person who leads an organization has earned a Ph.D. or a GED is irrelevant in terms of program effectiveness but can be a tough pill to swallow for those who cling to the idea the word *expert* only applies to those who hold a degree. Street Outreach Workers understand those they serve are the experts and treat them as such. When academia pushes their influence upon grassroots programs, usually leveraged in terms of funding channeled through the next wave of terminology that becomes the *next big thing* all programs must be trained in, it often comes from what academia has witnessed truly works through their research of grassroots programs, and those who have the skills to implement such programs. Academia may coin terms and create names for approaches and practices Street Outreach Workers have been successfully implementing for decades, but understanding the work from doing it, and understanding the work from doing research about it, is the difference between night and day.

You can attend any street outreach conference and witness the great sea of divide between those who think they know and those who know. The great sea of divide is experience. Experienced Street Outreach Workers, even when we respectfully attempt to inform someone from academia about the discrepancies in the materials they are presenting verses the reality of the streets, are oftentimes met with the words, *that's not what the research tells us*. There is no information more up-to-date and more accurate than the information directly obtained from those a program serves and those who deliver the services directly. If someone is truly an advocate who stands in solidarity with those they serve, not in words, but truly with them, the advocate will oftentimes find they are treated the same way as those they serve – marginalized and dismissed. This does not discourage Street Outreach Workers, it encourages us. There is no greater confirmation that we are truly following our calling in love and service than when society and institutions treat us the same as those we serve.

Narcotizing Dysfunction

Narcotizing dysfunction, a term from the book, *Mass Communication, Popular Taste and Organized Social Action,* by Paul F. Lazarsfeld and Robert K. Merton, is a theory that as mass media inundates people on a particular issue, they become apathetic to it, substituting knowledge for action. In this age of social media, I think it is safe to say narcotizing dysfunction is not a theory but a fact. It seems the masses truly do mistake having an opinion, liking, sharing or posting on social media for action, but it isn't. Every youth emergency shelter and domestic violence shelter is usually full. There are millions of homeless, runaway and sex trafficked youth. Yes, it's a pandemic. I am fortunate to work side by side, day and night with others whose mission it is to serve, yet the laborers are few. As programs that tirelessly serve others struggle to keep their doors open from year to year, I watch the news and see politicians generate millions of dollars in one evening of campaigning. People will pay $50,000 for a plate of food, listen to a candidate they support talk for an hour and take a photo with them, while we have children who are homeless, hungry, hurting and being bought and sold. Why is it that flyers of missing children barely get any shares on social media but a quote from a politician or professional athlete gets millions?

What came first, the marketing and branding or the consciousness of the masses? Either society has been overtaken by marketing and branding to the extent that money, sports and politics are what inspires ferocious passion in the masses, overriding common sense, compassion and the needs of those who are abused, exploited and marginalized, or the masses have always been shallow, and the marketers and branders simply followed suit. Why is there a media frenzy about missing sports jerseys, political ideologies, get rich quick schemes or religious differences, yet little coverage about the pandemic of missing, homeless, hungry, sex trafficked youth and victims of domestic violence? I think when someone acknowledges the pandemic of hurting, abused, and exploited youth and young adults it causes some to feel overwhelmed to the point where many think they cannot make a difference. It's almost as if the trauma that millions of youth and young adults endure creates a secondary trauma within others, causing others to take flight, fight or freeze, and the majority seem to freeze. It doesn't have to be that way. If everyone does what they can from where they are, a lot of healing will occur. We need to be more than lighthouses.

The Analogy of the Lighthouse is Ridiculous

Sometimes I will share an important lesson from an experience I have as a Street Outreach Worker on social media. Whether I share something on social media, when I'm facilitating a presentation or within this book, I don't share to tell you about all the good work we do. I share to tell you about all the work there is to do, and all the good you can do. I omit certain details and share a valuable lesson with the intention of encouraging others to do more. One time I shared such a post on my social media page about some challenging and heartbreaking events that occurred on the streets one evening. Shortly after I posted the lessons from that experience, I received a private message on my social media account. I opened the message and read, "Anthony, you do not understand that a lighthouse just shines. A lighthouse does not run all over the place trying to save sinking ships. The lighthouse does not talk about all the good it does. The lighthouse just shines. I hope one day you heed the wisdom of being like a lighthouse."

After I read that message, I was going to respond directly to the individual who sent it, but I learned long ago that getting into a disagreement with someone online is futile. I share what the Creator guides me to share, not hoping, but knowing it will get to those who need it. My response to that message is that analogy of the lighthouse for the times we are living in is ridiculous and dangerous. It is ridiculous because we are not lighthouses in the sense that we are human-made structures comprised of bricks, wood, electricity and a big light bulb. We are human beings comprised of minds, bodies, spirits and emotions. A lighthouse does not have hands, arms, legs, heart, spirit, emotions and a mind. If a lighthouse did have hands, arms, legs, heart, spirit, emotions and a mind, and all it did was shine a light on sinking ships while watching people die, then that lighthouse is not only useless, it's guilty of one of the worst crimes that has plagued humanity since the beginning – seeing, knowing, watching, yet doing nothing.

The analogy of the lighthouse is dangerous because it not only encourages doing nothing, it spiritualizes doing nothing.

Anything can be spiritualized and almost everything is, whether it pertains to Spirit or not. War, drugs, greed, violence, selfishness and doing nothing can be and are often spiritualized. We are not lighthouses. We are houses of *Light*, fortunate to have bodies illuminated and animated by *Spirit* with the ability to *move* with the Creator in love, service and leadership.

Cameras and Press are not Allowed

I cannot tell you the number of times I have been approached over the years by various news outlets and television channels from within and outside of the United States. And it still happens. There is a simple rule in all programs that serve youth and young adults who have been exploited: cameras and press are not allowed. Press may be permitted to speak with program staff about services the organization provides, but never with those a program serves, and especially not in the process of services being delivered. News outlets not being allowed anywhere near those you serve is obvious, or should be, for protecting confidentiality. Trust the Creator to send the word out about what you are doing. Those who are supposed to know about your services and are called to support the work you do will show up, eventually. Be equally diligent in honoring the confidence those you serve have given you.

At the emergency youth shelter where my office currently is, there are many people who periodically come to see the shelter. There is always the possibility someone will donate towards the needs of the children we serve, whether it is for the children who live at the shelter or those we serve through street outreach services. We need donations to do what we do, and we are forever grateful for those kind souls who show up and give in whatever manner the Creator guides them. Yet, this must be tempered with compassion by seeing the visits to our emergency youth shelter through the eyes of the children who reside at the shelter. We do not even call it a *shelter*, we call it a *home*, because that is how we keep it for the children. On more than one occasion, almost every child who has lived at our shelter has mentioned they do not like it when people come to see the shelter because they feel as if they are being put on display. The needs of those we serve come first, not the curiosity of potential donors or the bait that gets set by news outlets who always promise confidentiality, but their thirst for ratings seems to always override the proposed morals and ethics they present.

The most recent time I had a news outlet approach me was a few months ago. Some crew members from an international news channel invited me to dinner. I went because I wanted to hear them out and see if their angle was different from all the times before. I went to the dinner and the two reporters ordered their meal and I ordered mine. One of them, emphatically said, "Order whatever you want. The meal is on us." Of course, it was. While we were waiting for our meals, they shared that they really want to shine a spotlight on human trafficking and asked if they could go with me when I facilitate street outreach. They promised they would stay out of the way and only speak with the youth and young adults who are willing to speak with them, as well as blur their faces and change their voices on the recordings. My answer was no. Before I excused myself, I asked them to consider simply speaking with leaders in the field of human trafficking. Leaders such as clinical directors and executive directors of programs that serve survivors of human trafficking. Leaders such as special investigators in law enforcement and CPS (Child Protective Services), who can give them solid data and current trends. I especially attempted to steer them to the leaders who are survivors, now advocates, working within law enforcement and nonprofits. But no, they wanted something sensational like going onto the streets with me and filming on-the-spot trauma. From a Street Outreach Worker's perspective that is completely demeaning to those we serve and the work we do. Allowing cameras and press to be part of any process of the facilitation of healing severs the relationship between the Street Outreach Worker and those we serve; it also places the lives of those we serve, as well as the lives of Street Outreach Workers in danger.

Does Anyone Give a F**k About Me?

I have no idea how many suicide interventions the Creator and I have facilitated (It would be foolish to attempt such things on my own). There have been countless youth over the years who have handed me the gun, knife, razor or box cutter they were going to use to take their own life. It is never their life they are seeking to end, it's the pain. It is easy to tell someone *suicide is a permanent solution for a temporary problem*, and the person delivering such bumper sticker psychology does not see or does not listen to the fact the young person standing before them has been dealing with their struggle for twelve, thirteen, fifteen or eighteen years. I have watched adults deliver clichés like that to traumatized youth who have experienced endless pain, placements, systems and institutions for decades, but the adults delivering such clichés will lose their minds if their latte is not prepared correctly and ready in under five minutes at their local coffee shop.

Not long ago there was a girl who wanted the pain to end and felt the only way to do that was to die. She attempted to throw herself in front of a truck. I was there and was able to push her out of the way, but in the process, I fell in front of the truck. I thank the Creator the driver of the truck was

20

paying attention and swerved out of the way. I was able to restrain her until the police arrived with emergency psychiatric personnel who transported her to a psychiatric emergency hospital. In the three or four minutes it took for the police and emergency psychiatric personnel to arrive on scene, the young person kneed me in the groin while screaming repeatedly, "You don't give a f**k about me! Why didn't you just let me die?!"

After the young person was in the psychiatric hospital for a time, she returned to our facility and handed me a bracelet she made while in the hospital. The bracelet is beautiful and has letters on the beads that spell *I love you*. When she gifted me the bracelet, she shared, "I don't remember much about what happened by the road when we both almost died. I do remember telling you that you don't give a f**k about me, but what I meant to say is that I couldn't believe someone actually gives a f**k about me."

Until I gave that bracelet to a spiritual leader from the Tohono O'odham tribe in Arizona, I wore it every day. I wore it as a reminder about the Creator's miracle of saving our lives. I also wore it as a reminder that there are many youth and young adults who think no one cares about them. The job of the Street Outreach Worker is to prove them wrong.

From Mild to Extreme and Everything In Between

The calls Street Outreach Workers get and respond to range from mild to extreme and everything in between. An example of a mild call is a father and son who have been arguing a lot. After a brief, sincere, heartfelt intervention from the Street Outreach Worker, it's revealed the father and son both want the same thing. They both simply want more time together. The Street Outreach Worker helps them make plans to spend more time together and assures them services are available to assist them in the future if needed.

An example of an extreme intervention that became long-term services is when I was working with a teenager who was referred by juvenile probation to our gang intervention program. The young man was arrested for possession of marijuana and firearms. What wasn't in the referral or the file juvenile probation sent me, is the young person and his younger siblings were forced to watch the murder of their parents, then forced by the murderers to fight with them as child soldiers in Sierra Leone, Africa. He had never spoken with anyone before about the horrors he and his younger siblings endured, and the choices he had to make to save the lives of his younger siblings until he came to us.

The levels of trauma vary. There are no cookie-cutter situations or solutions. For the Street Outreach Worker it doesn't matter if someone endured or is enduring an experience others consider mild, extreme or anything in between. What matters to the Street Outreach Worker is that it is important to the person we are serving. Pain is subjective. It is personal, based on the experience of the person experiencing it. Someone in any room has the worst story to tell. Someone in any room has the best story to tell. The work, especially in group settings, is never about comparing pain, it's about sharing pain, and in the middle of the sharing, we discuss and find coping skills, build resiliency and slowly but surely, inch our way to post-traumatic growth.

If you have children, when something is important to them, it's important to you. When your child's heart is broken because their boyfriend or girlfriend broke up with them, you don't say, *that's nothing compared to what I've experienced. Let me tell you about real pain.* Okay, there are some parents who say things like that, but the depth of relationship they have with their children is questionable. The moment anyone, especially our children, have to question if their heart will be trampled upon when they share their feelings, part of that person is closed off. And so is part of the relationship.

We all learn and grow. If we make one, small positive change within our thinking each day, that is three hundred and sixty-five positive changes each year, which amounts to major, positive transformation throughout our lives. A Street Outreach Worker understands if something is important to someone, then it's important because that person is important. In this same light of thinking, if something is important to the Street Outreach Worker, then we honor that for ourselves. Honor, like the spiritual link of intention Street Outreach Workers are called to reach out to others from, is an inside job aligned with sacred intentions.

Sacred Intentions

Sacred Intentions

The sacred intention of Street Outreach Workers is love. One of the origins of the word *intention* is from a Latin noun of action, *intendere*, meaning to turn one's attention and stretch out. I think it's important to understand whatever our intentions are, is where we place our attention and stretch towards. When we are aligned, we pay attention to, and stretch towards what we are, which is love, thus experiencing more love. When we are misaligned, we pay attention to, and stretch towards what we're not, which is fear, thus experiencing more fear. Whether our intentions are aligned or misaligned, we experience either the love or the fear we are extending from and stretching forth, and that is what others experience when they're in our presence. We can choose, at any moment, to realign our intentions with love. In doing so, we see love everywhere, extending it – aligning and realigning with love in ourselves and others by reminding all those we are called to serve they are sacred blessings, miracles and gifts.

As you read this chapter, my hope is you don't just gain a better understanding of the sacred intentions of Street Outreach Workers but strengthen your own intentions more deeply in the love you are. And if need be, gently move from fear back to love so you can be a vessel of optimal service for the Sacred in whatever capacity you're called to serve.

Love & fear are Both Hiring,
Which Company Will You Choose?

When a child falls and hurts themselves, many surround them, help them up and help them heal. When an adult falls and hurts themselves, many surround them, point out what's wrong with them, try to decide if the person is worthy of help, and remind them about their fall.

The Creator of your understanding has chosen you and you have agreed to be here to do something only you can do. Through prayer and meditation, we can go deep within our hearts and get our own performance review from our *Boss*. As we review our job description with the Boss, we find our job description is our vision, mission, dreams and purpose. Our individual job descriptions may differ in *how* but the *what* is always the same, and the *what* in our job description is love. There is not one person, past or present, who our Boss has ever assigned the job of deciding who is or is not worthy. Our job is to love, nothing more, nothing less. If we find we have been doing things that are not in our job description, we are not doing our job, thus missing the mark and our calling. Perhaps we changed companies and didn't even realize it.

The only two companies we can keep and work for are Love or fear. They are both willing to have you work for them at any moment you choose. I assure you that you are much more qualified to work for Love. Besides, I heard an inside scoop that the more of us who decide to work for Love and accept the jobs of healing Love offers, the more others will, too. And in doing so, in just a little bit of time, fear will be bankrupt because in the spiritual economy, every investment in Love withdraws everyone away from the illusions of fear and all the jobs of destruction fear offers. I assure you Love is the right business because Love *is* your business.

Love is Your Business

There was a nineteen-year-old young adult who had been trafficked for many years. We were fortunate to find her and establish trust with her. She was extremely traumatized but allowed us to speak with her at a drop-in center. While the staff at the drop-in center fed her, gave her new clothes and allowed her to take a shower, we came up with several possible plans. After she was comfortable, fed, hydrated and relaxed, we sat with her and colored in coloring books together as we talked. We asked her what she wanted to do. The only thing she knew for sure is she wanted to be safe and never harmed again. We shared some of our thoughts about possible plans with her but wanted her to make the decision because she is her own expert, not us.

The young lady wanted to participate in a program about three hours away that specializes in assisting people who've experienced what she had. She didn't want us to transport her to that program until the following day. She was exhausted. But she did want to report everything that happened to her to the sex trafficking hotline that day. We followed her lead. The plan was for us to transport her to a local shelter, call the sex trafficking hotline on speakerphone with her to assist her in reporting everything she had endured, then the following day we would pick her up in the morning and transport her to the long-term facility three hours away.

While we were at the drop-in center, my street outreach partner got another crisis call and left to respond to that call. I took the young lady to the local shelter and assisted her in checking in. The shelter had a church inside and that's where she wanted us to make the call to the sex trafficking hotline. The young woman provided all the names of the predators who hurt her, as well as the gruesome details of what was done to her. The sex trafficking hotline assured us they would send the entire report to law enforcement in our area so they can begin an investigation. After the phone call, we processed her feelings about everything. She shed many tears and we prayed together. I didn't leave that shelter until she was at peace with me leaving.

After many tears and prayers, I left the shelter, and drove about four blocks when a car with four men in it cut me off the road and blocked me in. They didn't get out of the car, but the driver of the car looked me right in the eyes, and said, "You know you should mind your own business, right? You should really mind your own f**king business." Then they drove away.

I went home, initially shook-up, but after diving deep within prayer, I smiled and felt great. It's a wonderful feeling when predators don't like you. It's a clear sign you are on the correct side. The next morning we picked the young lady up from the shelter and transported her to the long-term care facility.

The abuse and exploitation of anyone is everyone's business. Predators love people who think it's not their business and hate people who know love is everyone's business. Predators count on instilling fear in those they prey upon, as well as others in the community. Predators love the *no snitch rule*, because it only benefits them. Love elevates us beyond fear and intimidation to take courage, even in the face of life-or-death situations because love keeps us focused on the truth, not the facts.

Love Keeps Her Focus on the Truth, not the Facts

Facts and truth are not the same thing. We have all witnessed two different people take the same set of facts and come up with two completely different truths. Although there is no universally agreed upon definition of truth, there are,

31

however, many versions of truth people arrive at depending upon how they place the facts together.

There are facts about any given situation that cannot be dismissed, however, when we are speaking about healing, transformation and the walk from the head back to the heart, it is imperative the facts of this moment be placed in a manner conducive to healing, not fighting against healing.

The facts of youth homelessness and human trafficking during these times we are living in as I write this book are astounding. These facts, which we all know very well, or at least have access to with one click on the internet, can be overwhelming, especially for Street Outreach Workers who can not only tell you all the facts as verified by academic research, but by our direct work in the streets. Those affected most adversely by the staggering facts are those experiencing them firsthand, right now, as you are reading this. As the saying goes, *those closest to the conflict are the experts.* When a youth, young adult or family is in crisis, they are not in need of experts. They need those who have answered the Creator's call of service to others and have the ability, whether from being formally trained, their own personal experience or a combination of both, to deliver them, in their most dire moments, to a truth that is bigger than the facts of the crisis they are experiencing.

The analogy I have used over the years, and continue to use when I facilitate presentations is with an apple. I will have a participant cut an apple in half, take out the seeds, count them, and tell all of us how many seeds are in the apple. If the participant tells us the number of seeds in the apple is seven, I tell everyone, "There are seven seeds in the apple. That's a fact." Next, I ask the participant to pick up one of the seeds, stand in front of the audience and hold the individual apple seed up for all to see. Then I ask the audience, "How many apples will come from this seed?" After scanning the audience for a moment, usually seeing a mixture of approving nods and perplexed looks, I share, "That's a truth. Facts and truth are not the same thing. No matter what we are going through in this moment, no matter how difficult the facts of the present circumstance may be, we must stay focused on the truth while we are dealing with the facts. We can only do that with vision."

We can literally perish in the facts of this moment if we are not encouraged by someone to keep our focus on the truth. There are many ways to perish. Hopelessness, despair, quitting, these and many other thoughts and emotions invoke death. We can all relate to one degree or another about hurt, pain, loss and tragedy, but the difference between focusing on the facts or the truth is the difference between life and death. Vision is what spirituality *is*. If you look at the lives of anyone

33

who has overcome adversity to persevere and actualize what the Creator has commissioned them to do, they kept their vision. The truth beyond the facts of the moment carried them above the situation, and eventually to what they refused to take their spiritual sight from, even if all those around them quit.

Creating Internal Metaphors

Street Outreach Workers meet the physical needs of those we serve by providing water, food, clothing, shelter and safety. After the physical needs are met, Street Outreach Workers use what's around us to help create internal metaphors for those we are serving. Although many of us have worked after-school programs and have vast experience in facilitating groups, workshops, and classes such as writing, poetry, theater, talking circles, t-shirt design, music, dance, martial arts, as well as coordinating and coaching after-school sports, Street Outreach Workers do not have the luxury of preparing, then implementing structured activities in controlled environments. Activities, in and of themselves, are not prevention or interventions. Activities, to the extent the person facilitating the activity can guide the youth and young adults in developing internal metaphors they can use outside of those activities, during very challenging moments, is where prevention and intervention occurs.

On the streets you must utilize what is at your disposal. The Creator is everywhere, always. The Creator provides every resource needed in every situation. Street Outreach Workers will be at a park, working with a young person who is homeless and afraid. As the Street Outreach Worker provides food, comfort and reassurance, the young person reveals they love to write and recite poetry. At the park, just twenty feet away are plastic drums on the playground, so the young person and Street Outreach Worker walk over to the drums and an impromptu poetry slam begins. Within the rhythm, rhyme and poetry on plastic drums in the middle of a park, pain is released, dreams are revealed, relaxation occurs, and preparation for the next step of the young person calling a safe family member begins. Safe family reunification occurs because the impromptu poetry slam reunified the young person with the Creator and their own heart in an activity they love. How can we do something we love without love being actualized?

A Street Outreach Worker goes by a local drug house to see if any youth or young adults are around. The Street Outreach Worker sees a young man sitting on the porch of the house and can tell he's been crying. The Street Outreach Worker and young man know each other. The young man immediately recognizes the Street Outreach Worker, gives the Street Outreach Worker a big hug, and shares, "I was just

praying, asking God to send me help, and now you're here."
The young man goes inside the drug house where he's been
for over a week, stuffs all his belongings into a duffle bag,
comes outside and the first stop the young man and Street
Outreach Worker make is the laundromat.

At the laundromat, the Street Outreach Worker helps the
young man wash his clothes. When the young man unzipped
the duffle bag, the stench of meth was so strong they both
dry heaved and almost vomited. After getting all the clothes
into the washing machines, the young man and Street
Outreach Worker walk across the street, order some tacos,
and bring the food back to the laundromat where they sit
down outside and eat. As they finish eating, the Street
Outreach Worker asks the young man, "So, what about the
meth pipe in your pocket?" The young man hangs his head in
embarrassment, realizing the Street Outreach Worker saw
him take the meth pipe from his bag and sneak it into his
pocket as they prepared to wash his clothes.

"I don't know. I don't know what to do with it. I don't
want it anymore, but I don't know how to live without it."

"Will you let me take you to a safe place where you can
live and learn how to live without it?"

"Yes. I think that's the answer to the prayer I was saying
today."

The young man and Street Outreach Worker go back inside the laundromat and place the young man's clothes in the dryer. They come back outside and sit down next to a tree. The Street Outreach Worker digs a small hole in the Earth, as the young man breaks the meth pipe on the sidewalk, gathers the pieces, then places the pieces in the hole. The young man lets meth and the meth pipe know all he loves and hates about them. The young man grieved through anger and tears, then buried the pieces. After the funeral service for his addiction, the young man and Street Outreach Worker went back inside the laundromat, folded his clean clothes and threw the duffle bag that was saturated with the smell of meth in the garbage. The Street Outreach Worker had a clean duffle bag in his vehicle, so the young man placed his clean clothes in a clean duffle bag, and the young man and Street Outreach Worker drove to an inpatient rehabilitation program where the young man was admitted and began to learn how to live again.

Even in an abandoned building, a Street Outreach Worker will create an internal metaphor for a young person who is thinking about ending her life. When I was inside an abandoned building looking for youth and young adults to serve, I found a girl who was going to kill herself. I prayed and asked the Creator for guidance. As soon as I prayed, my attention was immediately drawn to the broken mirror near the front door. I asked the girl if she would walk towards the front door of that abandoned building with me. She agreed, and we went and crouched down near the shattered mirror. We began to work with the broken mirror and did an exercise about seeing our true reflection through the brokenness – beyond the brokenness. After the exercise and a lot of processing, she allowed me to take her to a facility where she stayed for a time to get the long-term supports she needed.

Street Outreach Workers are not handing out rose-colored glasses. Street Outreach Workers deliver the Creator's deep, authentic, spiritual surgery within the minds, spirits, and emotions of those we serve, especially when it is not just a flesh wound.

Where is the Power?

It is always an honor when I am asked to come into a school, juvenile detention facility, or program of any kind to empower the youth. The truth is that it is impossible for me to empower anyone. Everyone has the power of life. Regardless of the hand we've been dealt, each of us can use all we've been given to make something good. For any excuse someone gives me, I can give them many examples of people in the same or worse situations, who not only achieved the goals and dreams in their hearts but achieved far beyond them. Instead of trying to empower the youth and young adults, I prefer to have them examine where power is. After they remember, we examine how they've been exercising it and how they can exercise it more intensely and more intently for their own well-being. I have entitled the exercise I use to do this *Sacred Choices*.

When I facilitate Sacred Choices with youth and young adults, I use a table with props, and it is always an amazingly blessed experience. I place a piece of tape across a table, and on one side of the tape I place props that represent each person's vision, mission, dreams and purpose. On the other side of the tape, I place props that represent drugs, alcohol and violence - things I refer to as *dream killers*. Then I ask, "Which side has the power?"

I intentionally steer the conversation to be controversial. When someone in the audience says, "The side with our vision, mission, dreams and purpose has the power," I ask, "Why?" After they explain their reasons, I inquire, "Has anyone here ever lost someone they love to the side of the dream killers?" There are typically many people who raise their hands. I continue, "Has anyone here only witnessed the power of dream killers in their lives, never experiencing the power of our sacred vision, mission, dreams and purpose?" Usually many people raise their hands.

After a moment of silence, letting things sink in, I ask, "Is there anyone here who thinks the side of the dream killers has the power?" Normally many hands raise when I ask that question. I call upon whoever is willing to express why they believe that and allow them to explain. At this point in the exercise there is tension and internal conflict with the participants. It is not uncommon to see tears well up in many of the participant's eyes. I press the participants after someone shares the side of the dream killers has the power, "Have you ever known anyone who struggled with dream killers, but because of a miracle they went to the side of their sacred vision, mission, dreams and purpose, and are now free from the dream killers?" Usually many people raise their hands because most have at least one person they know, or know of, who has had that experience.

After going back and forth for however long and in whatever direction the flow needs to be for optimal impact, I invite two people up to the table. One who believes the side of our sacred vision, mission, dreams and purpose has the power, and one who is convinced the side with the dream killers has the power. I have each of them stand on the side that represents what they think has the power while facing the audience. I thank them for their courage to participate, and instruct them, "On the count of three I want you to pick up one of the items that symbolizes what you think has the power and hold it up. One, two, three."

The second they pick up the items and hold them up, I emphasize, "Now it does! Neither of them had any power until you picked them up. Have you ever known anyone who walked by the liquor aisle in a grocery store, went to a different aisle and purchased orange juice, then left the store and killed an entire family because they were driving drunk? No. They would have to pick up the alcohol first for that to happen. Have you ever known anyone who shot and killed someone without picking up a gun? No. They must pick up the gun first for that to happen. Have you ever known someone who picked their books up every day, went to school, never missed class, did all their work, and did not get their education? No. They would never get their education if they did not pick up their books, open them and read them. Have you ever known someone who got high or overdosed on drugs without first picking up the drugs? No. Have you ever known someone who wrote a book without writing? No. Picking up the notepad or opening the computer, then writing each word, one by one, until the book is complete is how it happened."

One of the more hard-hitting examples I often use is, "Right now there is someone in a hotel room where a Bible is on or in the hotel room dresser, and that person is about to sell drugs or use drugs, sell a human being or use a human being, all with a Bible in that room. That Bible, although in the room, is not being picked up, thus not being lived. Until someone picks it up and lives it, it sits there, and the power being exercised is in what the person has picked up. I have often wondered if hotel room Bibles could speak about all they have seen, how many screams of horror have they heard? How many tears from children frozen by fear have they witnessed? A Bible, Quran, Torah, Eagle Feather, Drum, or any holy instrument used to commune with the Creator can just sit somewhere, never being picked up, so what we commune with is that which we consciously choose to pick up. What we consciously choose to pick up either awakens our consciousness with the Creator or dulls it. What we choose to pick up, especially in moments of pain and struggle, either alleviates our pain, struggle and lessens the dis-ease of doubt, guilt, fear and insecurity, or magnifies them. Depending upon what we pick up, we fall further awake in love or further asleep in fear."

I use those and whatever examples the Creator gives me to share for a while. Then I stand between the two volunteers who are still holding what they think has the power. I stand directly in front of the tape that separates both sides, touch that proverbial line, and share, "Every day, in each moment, we all stand on the line of choice in our lives. The choices of what we think and what we pick up. The streets will always be there. Drugs, alcohol, guns, knives, gang affiliation, and bad relationships will always be there. Dream killers are all around us. Some are legal and some are illegal, but they all detour us from our divine destiny. Our sacred vision, mission, dreams and purpose are not going anywhere, either. They're all around us. Most importantly, they're within us. Safely placed in our hearts for us to access and live or walk away from and pretend they don't mean anything, but even when we let go of what truly matters, what truly matters never lets go of us. So, if nothing on either side has any power until you pick it up, where is the power?"

Questioningly, the two volunteers along with the audience answers, "In us?"

"Yes. You! You have the power. None of these things have the power until you pick them up. When you pick them up, you are either enhancing the sacred power you have to actualize your vision, mission, dreams and purpose, which is the only place you will find true happiness, or you are giving your power away to the dream killers. Some of the dream killers may numb the pain for a moment, but in the end, exercising your power by giving your power over to the dream killers takes your power away. If you have the power to pick something up, what do you also have the power to do?"

"Put it down," the audience answers, almost every time, in unison. That is when I thank the two volunteers and ask them to put the items back on the table and return to their seats.

What do you pick up every day that keeps you close with the Creator?

What do you think you should put down that you pick up every day that takes you away from the Creator?

How are you using your sacred power to meet your needs and the needs of others in a way that is beneficial and healing?

What is Your Superpower?

Not long ago a friend of mine asked me, "If you could have any superpower, what would it be?" I thought about it for a bit and answered, "To disarm people. To have the ability to disarm a warlike mind and bring it to peace. The ability to disarm a person in front of me who is holding a weapon, not by force, but by love, so they hand the weapon over to me or place it on the ground and walk away from destruction and back to healing."

My friend laughed and shared, "That's why I asked you that. Don't you see that the superpower you want is the one you have?"

After we hung up the phone, I really thought about that. In contemplating our conversation, the realization occurred to me that we all have the superpower we want. We all have

the superpower the world needs. Super means *very good, excellent* or *pleasant*. Power means *the ability to do something or act in a particular way*. Now, placing both of those words together, *superpower* means *the ability to do something excellent in a very good and pleasant way*. There is no excellence in lying, cheating, stealing, slandering, manipulating, hurting or destroying. There is, however, excellence in truth, love, compassion, peace, understanding, forgiveness, hope, faith and charity. When you are willing to set aside your ego, which is nothing more than a confusion in your identity, and move from *who* you are back to *what* you eternally are, and reclaim your sacred vision, mission, dreams and purpose, you'll see the superpower you've always wanted is the superpower you have. And using your superpower, your gifts, is not a gamble, it's a sure thing when you share them.

Your Gifts are Not a Gamble;
They're a Sure Thing When You Share Them

Have you ever purchased a lottery ticket and then dreamt about what you would do if you won? Most of us have. We think how much easier our lives would be with the instant millions of dollars. We think about how many people we could help, especially those who have made sacrifices for us. It's fun to think about being able to be of more service. It is fun to think about how much more fun, joy and passion we

45

could have in our lives that instantly having millions of dollars could bring us. The fun of that fantasy all stops at the time they draw the winning numbers, then poof, the dreaming is gone. Imagination is disengaged, and the focus is back on the tasks of the day.

The big, instant dream of a huge avalanche of abundance pouring from a winning lottery ticket into our lives and out into the lives of others generates so many conversations about fun, future, giving and living. People can't help but join in the imaginings when asked, "What would you do with the money if you won the lottery? When asked that question, many people are momentarily filled with passion and can tell you in detail what they'd do, the changes they'd make, and how their lives would be better, if only by some remote chance they were holding the winning lottery ticket.

Years ago, I had a friend who purchased a Powerball lottery ticket and during the drawing their ticket matched all five of the first numbers, but not the Powerball number. He held that ticket in his hand and asked some of his friends and family in the room, "Did I win? Is this a winning ticket?" His family and friends assured him that he did not win anything. His family and friends convinced him, with complete sincerity, his $100,000 winning lottery ticket was worthless. His friends and family may have been sincere, but they were sincerely wrong. Nevertheless, he accepted their answers and threw his winning ticket in the garbage. A few days later, after doing his own research, he discovered he had won $100,000. It was garbage day in his neighborhood, so he hurried home in the middle of the day from work to pull all his garbage cans from the curb and go through each bag to find his winning lottery ticket. When he arrived home he saw the garbage had already been picked up, so he went to the garbage dump and knew his $100,000 ticket was somewhere in the middle of tons of garbage. He searched for hours in hopes of finding his winning lottery ticket. He never found it and was severely depressed for several weeks. After he came out on the other side of his depression, he was mostly upset with himself because in the moment he won, he didn't listen to his own instincts telling him he won. He listened to everyone in the room who told him his ticket was worthless. He allowed their voices to drown out the voice within him that was screaming, *they are wrong!*

Let me tell you a secret, *you are holding a winning lottery ticket.* A lottery ticket worth more than all the money the world can make. You may think your winning lottery ticket is expired, but it has no expiration date. You may think it is lost, but it is incapable of being lost. You may think it has been thrown away and destroyed, but it is incapable of being destroyed. It may be buried underneath disappointments, pain, loss, tragedy and the voices of some who say it's worthless, but it's there, in you, and it's priceless! Your winning lottery ticket is not something you can purchase, nor do you have to imagine all the passion, joy and benefits it can offer you, others and our world. You simply need to exchange it for all the benefits it holds. The only way to exchange it and extract all the greatness within it is by sharing it. Your winning lottery ticket, what you have to exchange for all the fulfillment and riches beyond money and material things you can possibly imagine is *you*. The real *you*. The *you* that is created in and with a deep, devoted and passionate vision, mission and purpose. You've been endowed by the Creator with every gift you need to manifest your vision, mission and purpose. Your gifts are not a gamble; they are a sure thing when you share them.

To exchange your gifts for all the benefits they can offer you, others and our world, the first person you must share them with is yourself, not dozens of people. If your vision is to write a book, begin writing the book. If your mission is to be a better parent, begin making one simple change that improves the relationship between you and your children. If your purpose is to obtain a degree or diploma, take the first step by registering for your classes. If you want to start a fire that will be a place of comfort, light and hope for yourself, others and our world, begin by gathering the matches and kindling, then lighting the fire in privacy - just you and the

Creator of your understanding. After the foundation of the fire is strong enough, slowly and surely, piece by piece, build upon the spark of the vision, mission, dreams and purpose you've been given. Allow your vision, mission, purpose and gifts to burn within you *first*, so you don't walk into a room full of people, light a match and allow someone to blow it out and say, "See? You don't have anything to offer." If you don't share your gifts with yourself first, you will make the same mistake my friend did. You will be in a room, holding a winning ticket, attempting to get encouragement and approval from others. But just like my friend, even when you are holding your winning ticket - your gifts - and all the evidence points to the possibilities of something remarkable happening, if you get caught up in external voices and don't immediately take the next steps in accessing what you've been given to share, others will intentionally or unintentionally try to convince you that what you've been given to share has no value. Your gifts are not a gamble; they're a sure thing when you share them.

Don't confuse your abilities with your gifts, because they are different. I cannot physically perform the martial arts now at age forty-seven as I could at age twenty-six. My physical abilities have dwindled a bit, but my gifts to inspire, motivate, teach, and allow the Creator to facilitate healing through me are eternal. Your gifts are not a gamble; they're a sure thing when you share them.

Just like people give themselves a moment to dream about all they would do with millions of dollars from a winning lottery ticket, give yourself a moment to dream again, in detail, about all you can do with your gifts. Then take the first steps in the presence of only yourself and the Creator. Your rewards, when you follow your vision, mission, dreams and purpose by utilizing all your gifts will be many. The most important reward you will experience is fulfillment. If you're living your life to *get* instead of *give*, then keep playing the lottery. If you want peace and fulfillment beyond understanding, that no amount of money could ever provide you with, then realize you've already won the lottery – you are the winning ticket! Look in the mirror and remember you are a sacred blessing, miracle and gift, fully equipped to be a blessing, miracle and gift to others. Success is not about how many people love your work, success is about love being your work, whether what you have been gifted to give is for one person or one million people. Whether or not you exchange your gifts and live your vision, mission, dreams and purpose is entirely up to you, but I guarantee you that someone, somewhere needs what you have to give. Your gifts are not a gamble; they are a sure thing when you share them. And when you share them, your gifts will light up the darkness.

Light Up the Darkness

In a holy instant, on the darkest of nights, the Creator sends a lightning bolt to streak across the sky revealing there's so much more than the darkness surrounding us. The glimpse that sacred light of love provides in the darkest times can be, and often is, the difference between life and death. Often, the Creator chooses to use people to be that light of love within the darkness for others. Sure, the Creator can, and does send help directly, without any intercessor, causing supernatural events to occur and we refer to those events as *miracles*. But what are you? You have a heart that beats without your help. Lungs that breathe without your thought. Blood coursing through your veins that continually provides life and nourishment to your body with no assistance from you. You have a mind, body, emotions and spirit. You have eyes to see and ears to hear. What do you see? What do you hear? Do you see and hear what the world shows you and tells you, or what the Creator reveals and speaks to you? Can you see that you are a miracle?

Vision is seeing clearly, and vision comes when our intentions are aligned with love. Do you see and hear yourself as the sacred blessing, miracle and gift you are? Or do you see and hear the lies that have been imposed upon you, breaking your heart repeatedly, causing you to lose the vision - the original dream you have been sent to live? Take courage. The

Creator has your back, and the time has come for you to realign yourself with the Creator, your beautiful heart and the great vision, mission, dreams and purpose you have been sent to this life to manifest.

All outreach begins by reaching within and remembering, then reclaiming what is truly you. The second step of outreach is extending your true self, the self that is eternally connected to and part of the Creator, outward to others.

The Truth of Peace

How are the children doing? The answer to this question reflects our society within our young people, not our young people within society. Our young people are the *answer*, not the problem. We have world peace day, world prayer day, red ribbon week, violence prevention week and a plethora of other days and weeks dedicated to good causes. But these events could be and should be lifestyles. When the most significant things are reduced to events instead of lifeways, our young people internalize this and follow our lead. What is honored in our society? What is lived daily in our society? What is the true message being conveyed by the adults in our society? Can we honestly say our daily actions, which is our true message to our young people, is love, faith, hope and charity, springing forth from the love we are and extending outward to others?

If we want peace, we must cultivate peace building. If we want to build something, the correct tools are required. Teaching our young people to use these tools daily is also required. The toolbox a peacebuilder carries is love. Opening the toolbox of love, we find the tools of compassion, empathy, selflessness, kindness, generosity, fortitude, forgiveness, charity, collaboration and humaneness. The toolbox of love is filled with the words *we, us* and *together*. The toolbox of love contains all humanity needs to build peace.

If it's true the opposite of love is not hate, but fear, then what would be within the toolbox of fear? What exists in the toolbox of fear is the exact opposite of love's tools. The toolbox of fear contains apathy, disdain, indifference, hatred, disunity, competition, greed, selfishness, being unforgiving, blame, jealousy, discontentment, condemnation, unwholesome reasoning, unskillful desires, self-righteous indignation, contrived malice, guilt and shame. The toolbox of fear contains everything needed for violence in all its forms.

Our toolbox is our heart and there can be no violence without fear. The root of violence is fear. The root of fearlessness is love. Before we can build peace, we must examine our tools and be honest about the toolbox we carry, because by our example our young people determine what tools are important based on the tools they witness us using.

Our actions show our young people what tools we deem important by the way we treat one another; the way we speak to and about one another, and by the way we love or fear one another. Our young people are more than willing to build peace upon this Earth with us, after they witness adults living peace as a way of life, not an event.

When our hearts are open, our intellect remembers love isn't conditional, compassion isn't partial, forgiveness isn't selective, unity isn't exclusionary, and peace is inevitable. Because when our hearts are open, peace is visible, not as a process, but as a decision. The holiest decision we can make.

In discarding the toolbox of fear, we remember the unshakable foundation of love, where the archway of peace exists for us to walk through. In taking this short walk from our heads back to our hearts, we remember, and can once again live the truth of peace.

How Can We Follow Something We Never Listen To?
Many people will tell you to follow your heart, but how can you follow something you never listen to? If you are willing to journey upon the sacred, seventeen-inch walk from your head back to your heart, you will align with and reclaim who and what you truly are. There are reasons people never take that walk. Some people avoid it, thus avoiding who they really

are. Others allow themselves to be held in straightjackets of labels that have been imposed upon them and labels they have imposed upon themselves, spending so much time judging themselves they cannot see themselves. Then there are those who willingly take the sacred, seventeen-inch walk from their head back to their heart. They hold hands with the Creator of their understanding and a trusted friend or mentor, and walk in love, prayer, laughter and tears. On this walk they experience some extremely painful moments but with a guaranteed breakthrough on the other side. That guaranteed breakthrough is breaking free from straightjackets of trauma that freeze us in moments of time. That guaranteed breakthrough frees us from negative labels and looping thoughts of horrific events to move from hopelessness to hopefulness. The work is difficult, perhaps the most difficult work there is. It is also the most important work there is. Introspection, looking deeply within ourselves in prayer and meditation to reclaim our vision, mission, dreams and purpose, then live them to the best of our ability is the payoff. A glorious payoff that offers happiness, joy and freedom. If you are going to be a vessel for the Creator to use to guide others on an extraordinary journey of healing, you cannot live your calling without doing the necessary, internal work required to keep you aligned in love. That way, when you find yourself on the razor's edge, love will guide you.

On the Razor's Edge with no Script

There are no scripts for interventions. Whether the intervention is for sex trafficking, drugs, alcohol, gangs, violence, homelessness or suicide, an intervention is truly walking the razor's edge. Interventions are often life-or-death situations. In situations where Street Outreach Workers find ourselves, there are minutes, sometimes seconds, to get someone to put down a loaded gun, drop a knife or box cutter, not jump into traffic, or make an exodus from a lifestyle that is certain to end in early death or incarceration. Street Outreach Workers would be foolish to believe we have the answers, but we walk securely in knowing the Creator has the answers.

There are three things necessary for me when I facilitate an intervention. The first thing I need is to make sure I am not the one who is facilitating the intervention. I get out of the way and pray, *Creator, You know what this person needs, not me, so please, You do this through me.*

The second thing necessary for me is a good sense of humor. Yes, interventions are a serious matter, however, never underestimate the impact of generating a smile or laughter in a crisis. Interrupting someone's negative pattern, just for a second, by asking the person if they believe in unicorns or if they think penguins have knees, can instantly cause someone to take a step back from the proverbial or literal edge and open the door to dialogue. Is humor always appropriate? No. Will humor always work? No. Having a good sense of humor simply means we're ready to share levity, joy and laughter at the right moments. Having good timing with humor comes from Divine guidance, experience, and lessons learned from mistakes. Having a good sense of humor also means, as Street Outreach Workers, we take our responsibilities seriously, but not ourselves. There have been numerous occasions, more than I can remember, when a successful intervention concluded with a young person telling me, through their laughter, "Mister, you're childish," as they made the decision to live.

The third thing necessary when the Creator and I facilitate an intervention, is the first words a person hears from me are *you are a sacred blessing, miracle and gift*. These are not mere words; it is as close as I can get to describe who and what the person truly is – what we all truly are. In a world where we are bombarded with reminders of what we're not, when someone hears a reminder of who and what they are, it awakens their truth. A connection is felt beyond the cognitive, interrupts negative patterns and opens the door to dialogue and de-escalation. Like being funny or knowing how to fight, an intervention cannot be faked. The words *you are a sacred blessing, miracle and gift* must come from deep within your alignment in love to reach the love the other person is, so they are instantly reminded of their pricelessness, grandeur and beauty.

We don't feel words. We feel the energy, intention and spirit that encapsulates words. The calling of a Street Outreach Worker utilizes every aspect of our being – mind, body, spirit and emotion. The energy, intention and spirit in which a Street Outreach Worker facilitates healing is aligned with love. That is why and how the facilitation of positive transformation occurs.

Storytelling is an ancient manner of sharing important information that helps us align our intentions. Storytelling is effective for many reasons. One reason is that important information is encapsulated within a story that connects the listener to what they already know and links them to what they think they don't know. In my opinion, storytelling is the best method of teaching and learning because every time a story is shared, new understandings are revealed depending upon our present circumstances and what stage of life we are in. I first heard the story of *The Sacred Tree* when my friend, brother, and world-renowned flute player, Kelly Kiyoshk, shared this story with a group of young people we were working with. This story has been passed down within First Nations communities for countless generations.

The Sacred Tree

There were three different groups of travelers walking along the same path at different times. Each of the groups of travelers carried offerings with them.

The first group of travelers came upon a tree they recognized as poisonous. Because they recognized the tree contained some poisonous elements, they motioned for everyone to go far around the tree, which they did. The first group of travelers offered *avoidance*.

Days later, the second group of travelers encountered the tree. They, too, recognized the tree contained some poisonous elements. This group saw the tracks of the first group that went far around the tree. The second group of travelers decided to tie a blue cloth to the tree to warn future travelers the tree was poisonous. The second group of travelers offered *labels*.

A week passed when the third group of travelers came into the vicinity of the tree. They saw the tracks that went far around the tree, as well as the blue cloth warning them the tree was poisonous. The third group also recognized the tree contained poisonous elements. But after much prayer and contemplation, the third group of travelers decided to make their camp around the tree. The tree became the center of their camp and they shared an entire season with the tree. They learned the poisons the tree contained could be transformed into healing medicines when cultivated with care, patience and love. The medicine the tree produced cured sicknesses that once had no cure. With honor, they approached the tree, and with equal honor they parted ways with the tree. Before they left, the group sang a thank you song and tied a red cloth under the blue cloth, marking the tree as holy - a significant reminder of the truth that Heaven and Earth are forever connected by the sacredness within all living beings. The third group of travelers offered *relationship*.

Because of the great courage only love can provide, the third group of travelers left tracks many others have been able to follow for healing. Because of love, the tree is no longer avoided or labeled, but sought for its truth of healing.

Avoidance, Labels or Relationships
The highest level of thought comes from the depths of our hearts. If it's not from the heart it holds no relationship to anything real. What we offer others, we offer ourselves. When we see healing, be grateful and certain it was cultivated. When we see poisons in others or ourselves, be equally grateful and certain in the choice of miracles. Only love knows how to cultivate healing. When we are willing to offer and receive love, we find within others and ourselves the answered prayers, purpose and miracles that have been with us all along.

We can avoid others, label others or we can spend a season with others and cultivate relationships. Relationships in love, truth, compassion and honor that will transform any poisons that have been imposed upon us into healing medicines. This is what outreach is all about. Outreach is not just about going out onto the streets and handing out food, clothing, survival bags, tents, sleeping bags, blankets, water and flyers with information about programs or ministries. Handing out those items to meet basic human needs is crucial, but those items must be a bridge linked with the intention of love. With the intention of love, a skilled Street Outreach Worker does not simply hand out supplies, shake hands and hope the person calls them when they need help. Street Outreach Workers understand the items we give others are an opening to meeting other needs, needs that have been frozen by trauma. Frozen needs, that love will thaw, so the sacred seventeen-inch walk from the head back to the heart begins. Sometimes that sacred seventeen-inch walk begins when we hear the right story at the right time, or when we're guided in an exercise that helps us rewrite our own story. One such exercise I facilitate with youth and young adults is something I've titled *Love Letters*.

Love Letters

An exercise I facilitate in small groups with youth and young adults, only after extensive work has already been done, is something I call *Love Letters*. We begin with a prayer and some deep breathing exercises to relax into the moment. All of us sit in the moment with some soft music playing in the background, a pen and paper in front of us, and begin to look within ourselves to find the person who has harmed us the most. After we've identified the person who has harmed us the most, we put them out of our minds. Next, we visualize ourselves in a beautiful field of green grass on a sunny day, sitting under and leaning against a huge tree that casts its beautiful, comforting shade over us. A light breeze caresses our face and rustles the leaves in the tree above us. Off in the distance we see a seven-year-old child running, dancing and playing. We enjoy watching the purity and innocence of the child as the laughter of the child penetrates our soul with joy. The child notices us and begins to skip towards us. The child walks up to us smiling, peering deeply into our eyes and heart. The child reaches in their pocket and hands us a letter. We realize the child is the person who had harmed us, long before they harmed us, when they were only seven years old. We write our love letters answering two questions: What would the seven-year-old version of the person who harmed

us tell us about themselves? What would they say to us about how they hurt us after they got older?

At best, this exercise leads participants to write letters of apologies from the seven-year-old version of those who harmed us, which leads to forgiveness that would have never been considered without the apology. At the least, this exercise provides a shift in perspective, leaving some breathing room for compassion to enter and begin to work in our lives. How often do we think of someone as a child, especially those who've harmed us, or even ourselves? There is a childlike purity and innocence in all of us, no matter what we've done or failed to do. Writing love letters taps into both the love we have to give and the love we have to receive. On the rare occasions when someone is unwilling or unable to participate in the exercise as outlined above, they write a love letter from themselves to themselves, which is something we should strive to make as part of our daily lives. We have the ability to make our lives a love letter to our families, communities, the world and ourselves. Make your life a beautifully composed love letter.

By the Grace of God, There Goes God

A few years ago, I was at a city council meeting where downtown business owners were petitioning the city council to pass ordinances that would push the homeless population out of town. I watched and listened, as one by one, each business owner went to the microphone and pled to the city council to pass the ordinances. What was fascinating to me was every business owner pleading for the homeless to be pushed out of town began their pleadings with, *by the grace of God, there go I*, as they briefly looked at some of the members of the community who happened to be homeless. The phrase *by the grace of God, there go I* has such depth and meaning if it's truly contemplated. I am not speaking about how most people use that cliché, and I am certainly not speaking about how the business owners were using that cliché. As I sat in that city council meeting, listening to that cliché being stated so many times within a two-hour sitting, I couldn't help but to think to myself, *Am I crazy? Is there something I am missing here? I am sitting here in the room with the homeless population. On the other side of the room are the business owners who won't sit with us or dialog with us, yet the only time they glance in our direction is when they say, by the grace of God, there go I.*

Street Outreach Workers say that cliché differently, because we understand it differently. When a Street Outreach Worker encounters a fellow human being who is suffering, we don't say *by the grace of God, there go I*, because we do not find gratitude in the suffering of others, we find gratitude in alleviating the suffering of others. A Street Outreach Worker will say *by the grace of God, there goes God, and I need to reach out and meet God again.* Street Outreach Workers understand God is within the person suffering and losing sight of that truth is losing connection with God. Reaching from God within us, outward to God within others is where communion - true prayer takes place.

If it is God you see within every living being you interact with, how can you not be driven with great passion by God within you to love and serve? The subtle but miraculous shift from *by the grace of God, there go I* to *by the grace of God, there goes God*, is where spirituality meets the streets.

Where Spirituality
Meets the Streets

There is nothing flimsy about spirituality and its application in this world. Spirituality is supposed to be practiced and lived as a way of life that creates a path of love, service and devotion to others. Years ago, when I was facilitating a gang intervention training, a person in the audience decided to share with me, "All the things you are teaching are useful, except for the spirituality stuff. The spiritual stuff isn't practical."

I responded, "Anything is impractical if we don't practice it. Gang intervention and any form of street outreach *is* where spirituality meets the streets to deliver the sacred fire of healing that thaws frozen needs."

Thawing Frozen Needs

Did the Cat Commit Suicide?

A beautiful cat was wandering lost in the wilderness on a cold winter night. Snow covered the ground as freezing temperatures, slowly but surely, began to disrupt her breathing, heart rate and instincts. When she first realized she was lost, she panicked and ran frantically in an unknown direction, hoping she would find shelter. Out of breath from running and discouraged from not finding shelter, her emotions began to grow as numb as her frostbitten paws. Her tears of desperation began to freeze to her fur, and with each struggling step, hopelessness began to fill her. Then, off in the distance, she saw a farmhouse. She mustered the last bit of courage and hope she had within her and moved towards the farmhouse. The weight of her despair, as well as the weight of the ice-covered snow sticking to her paws made her feel as if the weight of the world was upon her, because it was. Her world turned from the familiar place where she was born, grew up, loved and knew so well, to an unfamiliar, cold, dark place. With each shaky step she limped and cried out for someone to help her.

She was not experiencing a moment of weakness. She had just been strong for as long as she could. Despite all odds, she made it close to the farmhouse, where to her pleasant surprise, she saw the farmer's truck was just a few steps further. With her last bit of strength she crawled under the truck and felt warmth emanating from the motor. Warmth, oh, sweet warmth. The warmth gave her hope. Hope made her heart beat strong again. She leapt up, crawled onto the warm motor, and as her frozen paws began to thaw she knew she was safe. She curled up on the motor and fell into a deep sleep.

As he always did, in the morning the farmer awoke early. After he ate his breakfast and drank his coffee, he went outside, got inside his truck, put the key in the ignition and started the vehicle. The cat was instantly killed. Did the cat commit suicide? No. The cat was cold, lonely and afraid. The cat was merely seeking warmth, comfort and safety.

We all have needs. Sure, the basic needs of food, shelter and clothing are needs, but ask yourself, has your belly ever been full while your heart was empty? Have you ever experienced having all the things that bring comfort on the outside, yet within you, you felt so alone, even in the middle of a room filled with people, the loneliness was so intense it sent cold shivers down your spine? We have more needs than the basic needs of food, shelter and clothing. We need to be *seen, heard, believed, accepted, loved* and *safe*. We, as humanity, need one another. We are here to meet the needs of each other. It is a blessing and a responsibility to thaw the frozen needs of each other so we don't seek temporary warmth by curling up inside a bottle of alcohol, a bottle of pills, with a needle in our arms, or in a lifestyle that is not only destructive, but essentially suicide on an installment plan.

There are many people wandering lost in a cold, dark moment. Just one smile, one word of encouragement, one loving conversation, one afternoon with someone who cares, would shine a light of warmth and love so bright, their frozen needs would instantly thaw, pour out through their tears and rid them of their pain. What greater honor and purpose is there than to be there for one another, calling ourselves out of the cold, back to the warmth of the Creator and our beautiful hearts?

When We Are Seen

Until someone can see you as a sacred blessing, miracle and gift, they cannot see you.

The need to be seen is powerful. Do you remember a time when someone truly saw you? If you've had that experience you know how impactful it is. Some people avoid others and themselves. Other people label others and themselves. Street Outreach Workers see others with *vision*. A vision that looks beyond so-called mistakes, frailties, sickness and circumstances to see others as the sacred blessings, miracles and gifts we all are.

The power of someone seeing us gives us the power to see again. Our youth need new eyes to see. How can such an important and necessary gift be bestowed and received unless we see with sacred vision? Sacred vision is the result of aligning our hearts with the Creator. The purpose of any spiritual path is to awaken a new vision and open our hearts to the love we are. Once reclaimed, sacred vision is discernment and provides perspectives other people often miss. If you spend any time in the streets with a Street Outreach Worker, you will quickly notice when they are working with people, they have a keen sense of awareness, and seldom miss the subtle details that often eludes others. This vision is a sacred gift, available to anyone from the Creator to be used for love and service.

Our outreach team received a call about a family who was going to kick their teenage daughter out of the house. When our team arrived at the home, a CPS worker was already there. The mother was speaking very nicely to the CPS worker in English, but when she spoke to her daughter in Spanish, she said some of the most horrific things I've ever heard an adult say to a child. The mother obviously had no idea I understand Spanish. When I interrupted and asked the mother in Spanish why she was speaking that way to her daughter, her face flushed red and she didn't say a word for several minutes. I informed the CPS worker what the mother had said to her child. The CPS worker asked the mother if it was true. The mother didn't deny what she said to her daughter, but she was also unwilling to acknowledge there was anything wrong with what she said to her daughter.

The teenage girl was sitting on the floor, looking down as tears streamed down her face. She was silent and probably in shock as her mother, who was supposed to unconditionally love and support her, bombarded her with statements about her being a worthless whore whose life would never amount to anything. I looked at the teenage girl and said, "I want to tell you what you are." She cringed, probably from the thought that many of the adults in her life repeatedly told her she was worthless, and if she heard it one more time she would break or break someone's face. The girl was at her threshold and needed relief fast. I continued, "You are a sacred blessing, miracle and gift." As soon as I completed that sentence, she immediately looked at me and asked if we could go outside to talk while the CPS worker spoke with her mother. We went outside and the teenage girl told me everything. Through her tears, she told me about all the physical, sexual and emotional abuse she endured, and that she had contemplated suicide on many occasions. That girl had a long road of healing ahead of her, but she began to walk it that night with the loving support of others. She began walking her road of healing, not because she was told about all she *isn't*, but because she was reminded of all she *is*. She was seen, and because she was seen, she began to see herself again.

I challenge you to enter any school, youth group, detention facility, youth shelter or anywhere a group of youth and young adults congregate and ask them a question. Ask them how many of them have been told they will be dead or in prison before the age of eighteen years old. After you hold back your tears of sadness and anger when you see most of them have been told that numerous times, ask another question. Ask how many of them were told that by someone who was supposed to love, support and help them. I have asked those questions to countless youth and young adults across the United States. Without fail, every time I ask those questions, almost the entire room raises their hands. That's when I remind them those are lies and their destinies are not in the hands of the fears, doubts or rejections of others, but in the truth that they, as children of the Creator, are sacred blessings, miracles and gifts.

Street Outreach Workers do not see the youth and young adults as people who will be dead or in prison by the age of eighteen. Street Outreach Workers do not see the youth and young adults as the problem needing to be incarcerated, beaten or thrown away. Street Outreach Workers do not see the youth and young adults as victims, who at best, can only rise to mediocrity. Street Outreach Workers see the youth and young adults as the sacred blessings, miracles and gifts they are. Sadly and miraculously, in my experience, Street Outreach Workers are often the first people in a long time or ever, who have truly seen the youth and young adults we serve. Because Street Outreach Workers see them, truly see them with sacred vision, the youth and young adults begin to see themselves again.

When We Are Heard

Until someone hears you as a sacred blessing, miracle and gift, they cannot hear you.

I find it interesting that after a child is born the parents cannot wait until their child begins to speak. Then when the child begins to speak, sometimes the child is told to be quiet because the adults are talking. Many adults talk *at* youth and young adults, not *with* them. There seems to be a pervasive attitude in society that states because someone is older they have something more important to say, and that is simply not true. The youth are sent to this life with an important message. They are sacred blessings, miracles and gifts. When our youth and young adults know you see them as a sacred blessing, miracle and gift, they will entrust you with their voice, because unlike the countless other times they've been told to be quiet, they know you will hear them.

I encountered a young man in distress who was on the run. I received a call from a concerned citizen about a teenage boy who was sleeping in her backyard. The woman who called me was nervous and didn't know what to do. She gave me her address so I could go to her home and speak with her and the young man.

When I arrived at the caller's home, I found the teenage boy and the woman who called me sitting at her picnic table in the backyard. He had a blanket wrapped around him, as they both ate pancakes and eggs with orange juice and coffee. They were talking and laughing as I walked towards them. So many young people are not as fortunate as that young man to have a caring stranger look out for them. Walking up to introduce myself, the teenage boy's eyes went from open and cheerful to distant and nervous. He was getting ready to run. The intense shift in energy was obvious, and the woman who called me, asked him, "What's wrong? What's going on?" The teenage boy said nothing. He just glared at me, using every instinct in his being to assess what my intentions were.

I sat down next to the woman, not directly across from him, because he was already on high alert for a confrontation. It was obvious by his body language that fight-or-flight was on his mind. The other reaction to fear is to freeze but that teenage boy was no stranger to the streets and freezing just wasn't a reaction he had. I looked at him and smiled, "I'm not law enforcement or CPS. I am a Street Outreach Worker and this nice woman called me here to see if you need anything. Go ahead and eat. If you want, I can wait in front by my car until you finish your breakfast." His shoulders sank a bit as his breathing grew deeper, and although he still had suspicion in his eyes, he asked, "What is a Street Outreach Worker?" I explained the job a bit, which really interested him. At one point he told me he does everything I do with kids younger than him who he encounters on the streets. I complimented him on his loving heart and compassion, then asked him, "Where does your love and compassion, your need to ferociously protect those younger than you come from?"

Startled by my question, he looked at the woman for some type of reassurance. When I saw that, I interrupted, "Alright, let's cut the sh*t. I am here in both of your lives to bless you, not stress you. So, how long have you two known each other?"

The woman smiled, "He's been staying here a few days. His parents have money and know everyone around here. I called you because someone told me you might be able to help, but I don't want to get in any trouble."

"Okay. Cool. Now we're cooking with grease." I continued, "Again, I am here to bless you. I have a car full of food, hygiene products, blankets and water I can leave here, and we can just leave it at that. Or we can try to gain some traction on long-term solutions that will work for everyone, especially, you, young man."

His body language was much more relaxed, as he exclaimed, "You want to know where my protectiveness comes from? Here. It comes from here." He threw off the blanket that was wrapped around his shoulders, stood up, took his shirt off, and turned around so I could see his back. His entire back was filled with deep scars. Scars that looked like something you would see on a combat war veteran who had spent years in a prisoner of war camp being tortured.

He put his shirt back on, turned around, sat back down at the picnic table, and took another bite of his pancakes.

"What did he use on you?" I asked.

"How do you know the person was a *he*?"

"By the way you reacted to me when I walked up. Your eyes, breathing and tension just kind of all clued me in to knowing most of the pain that's been inflicted on you was by a man. Well, a male, because a real man wouldn't do that."

"He used a horsewhip."

"Who?"

"My stepdad."

"I am so sorry that happened to you. I am angry that happened to you. I want you to be safe and never experience that again. What can I do? What do you want?"

"I don't want to be home. It's not safe. My mom does nothing but cover up for him. Every time I told someone around here, they all know my parents and never even let me tell them everything that happened. They just interrupt me and tell me my parents are good people and would never do anything to harm me, and a lot of kids have things worse than me."

"I'm here. I'm listening. I hear you. I won't leave. And I won't say a word until you tell me everything that everyone else wasn't willing to hear if that's what you want."

After several minutes of silence and a nod of approval from the woman who had been caring for him, the teenage boy began to talk. He talked for hours. He talked about his childhood. How the divorce of his biological mom and dad affected him. How his biological dad not being in his life caused him great pain. How his mother's marriage to his stepdad changed his mom. She seemed to pick his stepdad over him and she not only ignores him, she denies the abuse he endured, even when he had to be taken to the emergency room. He talked about the good and bad. His pain, hopes and dreams. He gave a detailed account of all the abuse he suffered, as well as the good times he remembered. When he finished talking he was exhausted but relieved. He told me he'd never been able to say all those things before. He reiterated that every time he tried to share all those things he was interrupted, and the conversation, like the help, hope and healing he needed, was hijacked.

With his permission, I left the picnic table, made the phone calls I needed to make, routing every contact I have in law enforcement and CPS to wrap around him, protect him and deliver him from the hell he had been living for so long.

He was placed with safe relatives where he is happy and thriving.

I am a mandated reporter, so I would have made those phone calls even without his permission, but for me, getting permission from the youth I serve is important. It includes them in their healing process instead of just more adults telling them what they need. When the youth are included in the process they are acknowledged as the experts of their experiences, which lets them know they are being heard. When a young person knows your only intention is to help them, and you truly hear them, this reconnects them with their own powerful voice.

Street Outreach Workers want to hear the voices of youth who've been unheard. The voices that have been beaten back into the recesses of their minds. The voices that have been hidden for so long out of fear their voices would be scrutinized, disrespected, mocked and rejected again. The voices the youth and young adults forgot they even had until someone was willing to hear them again. Through a Street Outreach Worker's ability to listen and skillfully use the power of silence, they walk the youth and young adults through the internal abyss of pain, loss and tragedy, shining a powerful light of listening upon words the youth and young adults thought were lost. Street Outreach Workers unravel the voices of strangers, illusions and lies, gently removing them, so the youth and young adults once again hear their own voices recall and reclaim the sacred blessings, miracles and gifts they are. Because Street Outreach Workers hear them, truly hear them, the youth and young adults begin to hear themselves again.

When We Are Believed

Until someone believes you as a sacred blessing, miracle and gift, they cannot believe you.

Have you ever dug deep within your heart, gathered all the courage you could find and spoken a truth so painful, it not only made your voice shake, but your soul shake as well? Some say we are only as sick as our secrets, and that is true on many levels. Regardless of what we achieve and outward appearances, if we are not honest with ourselves, healing proves to be challenging. I have shared with countless youth and young adults that I don't care if they lie to me, but I never want them lying to themselves. Lying is a survival skill for many of the youth and young adults we serve. At an early age, many of them learned that telling the truth brought them immense pain. When a child knows you see and hear them, they are much more willing to break the three rules that exist in all unhealthy relationships: Don't talk. Don't tell. Don't feel. Whether the unhealthy relationship is a negative work environment, a strife-filled marriage, or criminal and trauma-filled situations such as the abuse of children by sex traffickers, gangs, and the johns and janes who purchase children for sex, all those situations contain the same rules of don't talk, don't tell, and don't feel. When anyone, especially a child who has been directly and indirectly told they don't have a voice is willing to talk, tell and feel, it is crucial to believe them. If the investigation process reveals there are things untrue or embellished in their story, fine, that can and will be dealt with by incorporating it into the healing process. Not believing them, at least for a Street Outreach Worker, is never an option.

I received a call from a school counselor about a teenage girl who walked to the school and wound up in the counselor's office. Initially, the girl went to the school to enroll in classes and continue her education. As the school counselor spoke with her, she divulged she was living in an abandoned trailer a few miles down the road. I arrived at the school and the school counselor and I unfolded the situation with the child.

The teenage girl had not only been living in the abandoned trailer by herself, she had been placed there by her dad and stepmom who thought it would be an appropriate *scared straight* type of environment where their daughter would learn to be respectful. The girl had not had anything to eat for several days, so she was eating a lot of food with the school counselor before and after I arrived. The school counselor and I called CPS and made the necessary reports. I transported her to our emergency youth shelter. On the way to our emergency youth shelter she took me to the abandoned trailer where she was forced to live as a punishment. The trailer was on a lot of land owned by her stepmother. I had the child wait in my vehicle as I went inside the trailer. It was just as she described. There was no insulation, food, toilet or running water. There was nothing other than a plywood floor and a sleeping bag. I took photos of the inside of the trailer as part of the documentation process.

After she settled in at our emergency youth shelter and her basic needs were met, she began to tell me about the reasons her dad and stepmother placed her in the abandoned trailer. She told me her stepmother had been very abusive, both physically and emotionally, and she got in trouble anytime she told her dad about what his wife was doing. The other thing her parents considered disrespectful was sometimes she ate food in her room and forgot to clean the dishes.

Eventually, when I met her dad and stepmother, they both confirmed exactly what the girl had told me. Without hesitation, they both let me know if CPS gave her back to them, they would take her right back to the abandoned trailer.

At first, her parents were willing to relinquish custody of their daughter to the state, but found out that relinquishing their parental rights included having to pay child support to the state, and their financial status was important to them. I tried to explain to them their daughter was not doing anything bad, yet what they were doing is mental, physical, emotional and spiritual abuse. They refused to acknowledge the torment their daughter had suffered and that they were the perpetrators of her suffering. I thought with all the documentation, photos and the parents' unwillingness to acknowledge any wrongdoing, receive any help or make any changes, it was just a matter of time before CPS took custody of the girl.

A few weeks later I received a call from a CPS investigator informing me the case was closed with no wrongdoing found on the part of the parents. I was shocked. I pleaded with the investigator to take the time to look at all the evidence again, including the sworn statement of the parents that confirmed everything the child had said. I spoke with the CPS supervisor and called the initial investigator multiple times, all to no avail. After a few hours of being on the phone with CPS officials, I received a call from the girl's dad telling me he would pick up his daughter the following morning. There was nothing we could do. CPS closed the case and the girl's legal guardian could pick her up and take her home.

When the girl returned to our shelter from school that day, I informed her of all that happened and that she would be picked up the next morning by her dad and stepmother. She shook, cried and had difficulty breathing. The staff and I helped her through that moment, assuring her we believe her, and guiding her through breathing and grounding techniques. We informed her that we would always believe her and will always be here to help her. We also shared with her that she should never hesitate to call 911 if she was being abused. And if her dad and stepmom took her back to that abandoned trailer, she should immediately walk to the school and the school counselor would call me and we would start the process over again.

The next morning at 10:00 a.m. her dad and stepmom picked her up. At 11:30 a.m. I received a phone call from the school counselor telling me she was back at the school because she was dropped off at the abandoned trailer again. I went to the school and the school counselor and I called the police and I contacted a CPS worker who I knew would do anything and everything to ensure a child is safe. The police and the CPS worker arrived at the school. The police took the report while the CPS worker was making phone calls and documenting everything. The CPS worker received a phone call from his supervisor who told him to leave the situation because he was not dispatched there by CPS, but came to the scene by responding to my personal call. Before the CPS worker left the school, his supervisor called back and asked to be put on speakerphone with me. His supervisor asked me my take on the situation. I informed his supervisor what was happening to the girl was unacceptable and they should have never closed the first case. The supervisor said he thought the dad and stepmom were good people and informed me the dad was on the line with us on a three-way call. I was a bit surprised but didn't waiver in advocating for the girl. I shared that the parents admitted to physically harming the child, placing her in an abandoned trailer, said they'd do it again, and they did! The supervisor asked the dad if he'd be willing to allow me to transport the girl back to our emergency youth shelter where she could stay again while CPS conducts another investigation. The dad agreed. I transported the girl to our shelter, and again, on the way to the shelter we stopped by the abandoned trailer, which was in the same condition as before, and I took more photos for documentation.

The girl was back at our facility for a little over two months. She was going to school, getting all A's in her classes and was a peer mentor at our shelter for other kids. She thrived at our shelter. She was with us during the Christmas holiday. On Christmas morning, I woke up and the Creator prompted me to go to our shelter, call the girl's dad and stepmom to invite them to the shelter and offer them a Christmas gift. As soon as the Creator prompted me to do that, I knew what I was being asked to do. On December 17, 2016, just a few days before Christmas, our eldest daughter, Kelin, unexpectedly passed on at the age of twenty-three years old. Kelin wasn't sick and thankfully my wife and youngest son were in Honduras with Kelin when she passed on. It was and still is devastating. But as always, if we are willing, the Creator can and will transform *any* poison into a healing medicine.

As I drove to our facility I began to doubt what I was doing. How in the world could the Creator be asking me to go and plead with the girl and her parents to turn their hearts back towards each other by sharing what my family, just days before, had gone through? Well, as always, the Creator's word is confirmed. As I pulled into the driveway of our facility I saw the girl's dad and stepmom had just arrived. I got out of my car and told her dad, "The Creator had me come here to give you, your wife and daughter a Christmas present."

He looked puzzled, "Okay, we're here to give our daughter a book," he shared.

We walked inside the shelter and I asked the girl if she'd be willing to come to the office to speak with me and her

88

parents. She reluctantly agreed, and we all sat down. I also asked two of the shelter staff to come inside the office as witnesses. We were all there and the girl's dad handed her a book. The girl thanked him and her stepmom. Then it was my turn.

"I am not here in any counseling or therapeutic capacity right now. I'm here to give all of you a Christmas gift with the only thing my family has to offer at this moment. Our oldest daughter passed away a couple of days ago." I began to sob and started to think the parents of this girl did not deserve my tears or this gift, when I heard the Creator whisper, *just do what I asked you to do and don't worry about how they react. Leave everything else up to Me.* Through my tears, I bellowed, "All we have to give you right now are our tears and broken hearts. I am laying them before you to use as a bridge to walk back towards the Creator, your own hearts and each other. Please! When someone passes on, the veil drops, making it very clear what's important and what is bullsh*t. You both have an amazing daughter and I know somewhere inside each of you, you know she is in your life for you to bless, cherish, honor and protect. Please search within yourselves and find the Creator's voice telling you what I am saying is true. Please begin your healing and don't hurt her anymore. Don't abandon her anymore." I'm sure I said other things but at that moment I was moved in such strong conviction by the

Holy Spirit, and when that happens I don't always remember everything that is being spoken through me.

There was no discussion about what I shared. There wasn't even a pause of reflection by the girl's dad or stepmom. He looked at me, "Mr. Tony, I'm sorry about you and your wife's daughter, but I am not into all that emotional sh*t." He looked at his daughter, told her Merry Christmas, then he and his wife left our facility. I wasn't in shock. The Creator prepared me for that moment. At that moment I truly had the grace of peace that surpasses understanding. The girl thanked me and shared she already received the gift of walking back to her heart the first time she was with us because we believed her.

A few weeks after Christmas I received a call from CPS telling me they had closed the case because they found no wrongdoing on the part of the parents. This was the second time the parents admitted everything their daughter said was true. Twice, CPS found no wrongdoing on the part of the parents by grabbing her by the throat, pushing her into walls, and placing her in an abandoned trailer with no food, water, toilet, shower or insulation. The dad was on his way to the shelter to pick her up. The girl was terrified. She asked all the logical questions as I sat with her having no answers. She wanted to pray, so we did.

Her dad came and picked her up. A few hours later I received a call from the girl. She was about an hour away in front of a church where her dad had dropped her off. Her dad told her if she went inside and signed in she would be part of their program. The dad had filled out all the paperwork, but the girl hadn't gone inside yet, so she hadn't signed any paperwork. She told me the pastor wanted to speak with me before she went inside and signed anything. I drove to the church and met the girl and the pastor outside. The pastor shared, "There is nothing wrong with this child. However, there seems to be a lot wrong with her dad and stepmom. Yes, her legal guardian signed the paperwork and left without saying a word to this precious girl. I have no obligation, legal or otherwise, until she walks through the doors of this church and signs the paperwork as well."

Turning to the girl, the pastor asked, "What do you want to do?" The girl told us about a family who loves her and treats her well. She said she wanted to live with them and they want her to live there, too. The pastor nodded at me, and we took all the girl's belongings to my vehicle and I drove the girl to the home.

She is doing great. She graduated high school and is attending college. As for her dad and stepmom, they seemed to miss all the times and signs the Creator afforded them to change their course. Months after placing the child with a safe family, we saw on the news that both of the girl's parents are in jail on capital murder charges.

Thankfully we believed the girl when she told us her experience of abuse. Only the Creator knows for sure, but she could have been in the middle of things, or even a victim when her dad and stepmom decided to commit murder. But she wasn't, because she was fought for and believed. Now, most importantly, she believes in herself.

The youth make many outcries, many of which would go uninvestigated if a Street Outreach Worker does not advocate for the youth or young adults. Street Outreach Workers see, listen to, and believe the youth and young adults. Street Outreach Workers show the youth and young adults how to talk, tell and feel. Because Street Outreach Workers believe the youth and young adults, the youth and young adults begin to believe in themselves again.

When We Are Accepted

Until someone accepts you as a sacred blessing, miracle and gift,
they cannot accept you.

I think the words *respected* and *accepted* rhyme because they go hand in hand. You can unconditionally accept someone without accepting unacceptable behavior. Understanding that turns the dial, ever so slightly, even one degree, and transforms someone from a person who just watches kids and makes sure they don't get hurt, into a healer, a *transformation specialist*. Acceptance, like respect, isn't something to be earned, it's something to be given, and giving it is how we know if we have it. Never underestimate the power of acceptance.

There was an eleven-year-old boy who was in our program and did amazing. Sure, there were moments he was unwilling to follow the rules and had to be redirected by staff. If the redirection was applied with love, compassion and an explanation as to why the rule is important for his safety and the safety of others, he had no problem turning his behavior around. We were the first group of people in a long time he listened to, and he listened to us because we accepted him. Eventually he left our program and went to reside somewhere else.

He didn't receive the same unconditional acceptance at his new placement, so he ran away from that placement and lived on the streets. It didn't take long for predators to get to him. He became a victim of sex trafficking. He was eleven years old and had been trafficked by predators who kept him drugged as they repeatedly raped and sold him. For months, law enforcement along with Street Outreach Workers looked for him. When law enforcement finally found him, his dress, speech and demeanor made him almost unrecognizable. The trauma he endured is not something I am going to write about. What I want you to know is when law enforcement found him, he was unwilling to speak with anyone. He was physically combative with law enforcement and was only willing to go to one place - back to our program. In the middle of the ground zero trauma the eleven-year-old boy was experiencing, the only safe place he was willing to go was with us. He was willing to come back to us because we accepted him unconditionally. He came back to us for a time and because he knew he was unconditionally accepted, he was open to allowing us to guide him to invest in himself by allowing others to take him to a long-term placement that specializes in serving child sex trafficking survivors.

Because a Street Outreach Worker saw him, heard him and believed him, he knew he was accepted. He didn't have to prove anything. The acceptance didn't depend on his attitude, behavior or grades. Before he met Street Outreach Workers he was accepted only if he followed the rules. Street Outreach Workers never place rules above relationships. He is on the healing road, knowing he has a long way to go, but also knows unconditional acceptance. Because Street Outreach Workers accepted him, he began to accept himself as the sacred blessing, miracle and gift he is.

When We Know Others Have Faith in Us

Until someone has faith in you as a sacred blessing, miracle and gift, they cannot have faith in you.

Have you ever made a mistake? Of course. Will you make more mistakes? Certainly. We are perfectly imperfect human beings. We are here to love, be loved, and serve. Even when our intentions are aligned with the Creator of our understanding and our beautiful hearts, we make mistakes. When we do, do we just give up on ourselves and lose all faith in who and what we are? No. We take the time to learn from our mistakes. We process what we could have done differently and what we can do better. Yet, for some reason in our society there is the notion that mistakes are fatal. Mistakes are not fatal; they are necessary, unavoidable indicators we are getting results, although it may not be the results we want. We adjust and keep moving forward. However, there are systems and expectations in place that burden our youth and young adults with the pressures of perfectionism. High standards are one thing, but perfectionism steals our joy and blinds us to the amazing things we have accomplished, because when we are running a pattern of perfectionism, we contrast any accomplishment with the notion of *perfect*, and demean or dismiss our own progress. This leads to being hypercritical of ourselves and others. I have never met someone who was hypercritical of themselves that was not hypercritical of others. That is a horrible cycle, and to a greater or lesser extent, most of us have experienced this.

I had the honor of working with a young man who had been through many traumatic events in his childhood. Despite all the trauma he endured, he held steadfast to excelling in school and athletics. Then, one day, his dad walked out of his life and the young man turned his back on everything and anything positive. When he exited all positive endeavors, this created a vacuum within him, and he eventually became a member of a highly organized gang.

One blessed morning I was given a file from juvenile probation stating the young man was now in my program. I set the file aside on the pile of other new intakes I would be conducting that evening during street outreach and proceeded to complete some other paperwork. As it came time for me to go out into the night, I reviewed my new intake files. The young man lived right around the corner from our home. I knew who he was, and he knew me. Since the young man's home was right by ours, I called and asked his mother if I could come by late as my last stop of the evening. That worked out great because the young man's mother didn't get home from work until 11:30 p.m. We agreed to meet at their home at 11:30 p.m., and his mother agreed to make sure he would be there.

I arrived at their home and as soon as I walked in, the young man smiled, "Tony? Sh*t, man, I knew I'd be working with you one day." His mom yelled at him for cussing as she handed me a cup of strong coffee. We sat down, filled out the paperwork and came up with a six-month game plan for the work the young man and I would be doing together. We went over his goals and how we would achieve them. It was a great initial meeting, but we all knew the coming months weren't going to be all smooth sailing.

During the first three months of our work together the young man was compliant with all the terms of his probation, but there were no signs of transformation. As I already stated, we lived around the corner from each other, so I knew what was happening in our neighborhood. He had managed not to get in trouble with law enforcement during those first three months and was testing negative for drugs at his probation appointments. He had no curfew violations, not even when juvenile probation conducted late-night curfew checks. Then one evening, a police officer called my phone telling me they had one of my kids with them and asked if I would be willing to come meet them. I told the officer I would be there. When I asked where they were, the officer informed me they were just a few blocks away from our home. They had the young man detained just up the street from our house.

I got up, went down the street and saw the young man in handcuffs sitting on the curb as two officers were trying to talk with him. There were several other officers on the scene arresting many other young adults and some older men. As I walked up, the officers explained to me that all the others were arrested for drug possession and firearms charges. They also informed me that although they could have arrested the young man, they knew he was in our program and heard about the progress he was trying to make. The officers were considering allowing me to take him home instead of arresting him.

The young man went off. He started yelling, "Tony, see? See how these racist cops do us? They just came up and started harassing us for no reason. One white cop and one black cop that just don't like Latinos."

Extremely frustrated, I responded, "Are you kidding me? These two officers called me when they could have you in a squad car right now on your way to jail. Besides, you said they are racist. Everyone knows what happens here on this corner, at this time of night. I'll just say it without saying it. You say these cops are racist, but what group of people are the majority here in our neighborhood?"

"Latino," the young man responded.

"And the majority of the people who come to this corner to buy drugs are from here, in our neighborhood, correct?"

"Yes."

"So, you are proud to be Latino, but you're selling sh*t that kills people to mostly other Latinos, our neighbors, and these cops are the racists?"

"That's f**ked up, Tony."

"You're right! That's real f**ked up! That aside, you've figured out a way to successfully sell a product that kills people. Just imagine the kind of success you'd enjoy if you offered something that heals people."

The officers told the young man the same things that me and many others have told him. They told him they saw so much potential in him and if he just made a few difficult, but positive changes in his life, it would mean the difference between living his dreams or being incarcerated with his other associates. At that point the young man wasn't saying a word. His eyes were welled up with tears and I couldn't tell if he was on the verge of crying because he was in a rage with the possibility of going to jail, or if there was a breakthrough happening.

The officers went off to the side and had a conversation between themselves. They came back over to me and the young man, had the young man stand up, took off the handcuffs, and told him, "Tonight you're going with Mr. Goulet. If this happens again we're taking you directly to jail." I took him home and although it was a short distance, we didn't say a word to each other. As he walked inside his house, I told him, "I'll be here tomorrow night at 6:30 p.m. to pick you up for the gang intervention group." He didn't respond, and I had doubts he was going to go with me to group next day.

I went to his home the next day at 6:30 p.m. He was waiting on the porch, walked directly to my car and got inside. We processed what happened the night before to and from the gang intervention group. He seemed to have gained some strong insight that he was standing at a fork in the road, and his next decision would make a huge, lasting impact on his destiny. As always, there is the *why* behind the *what*. He let me know he made the decision to go and hang out on that street corner because his dad called him and told him he wanted to start spending time with him again. That really got to him and he was extremely emotional. He didn't know what to do, so he went and did what he knew, not necessarily what was right and safe, but what was normal. That's where the progress of transformation began with him – getting to the root cause. Gangs were not his first choice, his dad was, and once we began processing and working with that, he started to make huge strides.

He was going to groups and doing the deep, challenging, internal work transformation requires. He was experiencing breakthrough after breakthrough. His grades went from failing to all A's and B's. He was working a part-time job after school. His mother and sisters could not believe how much he had changed for the better. He did some forgiveness work about his dad and was speaking with his dad regularly by telephone because his dad lived in another state. He told me his dad was going to drive out and they planned to spend a weekend together to catch up in person. He was excited about that, at least until that weekend came.

The young man called me on a Sunday evening explaining he was tired of trying, because even when he did things just seemed to go wrong. He said he might as well do what pays well and live life to the fullest instead of playing by some bullsh*t rules and keep getting let down. He was discouraged because the visit with his dad did not go well. They mostly argued for the brief time they were together. Although the young man did a lot of his own deep, internal work, the dad was nowhere near ready to meet the young man where he was on his healing journey. He hadn't seen his son in almost six years, yet he demanded respect from his son that he was unwilling or unable to give to his son.

The next day was the first time the young man was a no-call, no-show with me in all the time we worked together. I went about my day and facilitated outreach and groups. A few days later, I received a call from his probation officer telling me the young man had been arrested for having smoked half a blunt and having the other half of it on him when the probation department did a curfew check. The probation officer told me the young man had court that afternoon. I went home, put on a dress shirt and tie, and went to the court hoping the judge would allow me to share about the young man's progress.

When they brought the young man into the courtroom in shackles, he saw me and looked both embarrassed and happy. When it was his time to face the judge, his probation officer informed the judge I was there to share some insights about the young man. The judge allowed me to speak and I began to share all the young man's progress with the judge. I acknowledged the young man did violate the terms of his probation by being in possession of and smoking marijuana. I also explained the situation about the young man and his father, and that the young man was self-medicating with marijuana. I told the judge I was willing to work with the young man more, specifically in the areas of relapse prevention and positive coping skills.

The judge kept reading the young man's file, looking up at the young man and then back down at the file. It was an intense few minutes of private deliberation in the judge's mind, and none of us knew what the outcome was going to be. Then the judge spoke. The judge yelled at the young man about his probation violation and told him that with his past criminal history he was surprised the young man was sent to a program like mine. It was not looking good. Then the judge softened his tone a bit and acknowledged that compared to all the criminal charges and behavior the young man had before, smoking half of a blunt was minimal. And although by the letter of the law it justified incarcerating him, the judge began speaking about the spirit of the law and how progress looks different depending on where we are at in life. The judge freed him but added six additional months to his probation.

Shortly after that day the young man and I discussed his desire to leave the gang. He was in a highly organized gang, one that does not normally allow anyone to leave, at least not in one piece. The young man, due to his history and rank within the gang, thought the leaders would allow him to be blessed out. Thankfully, he was right. He bravely went to them and let his request be known, which could have cost him his life. They blessed him out without any harm to him or his family. The downside was the young man no longer had the backing of the gang and still had a long list of enemies from rival gangs who could care less if he was officially in or out of gang life. Which is another reason why leaving a gang is courageous on so many levels, levels only those who've done it can truly understand.

I asked him, "What made you take that huge, courageous step of leaving the gang?"

"People kept having faith in me, Tony. Even when I didn't have faith in me, I kept running into other people who had faith in me. I expected my mom to have faith in me. Sh*t, I expected you to have faith in me, and that helped. But when I came across cops and judges that had faith in me, it just kinda all came together."

A Street Outreach Worker saw him, heard him, listened to him and believed him. A Street Outreach Worker didn't just ferociously advocate for him. The Street Outreach Worker, a couple of police officers and a judge saw *greatness* in him. We all had one thing in common – we had faith in that young man, and because we did, he began to have faith in himself.

When We Know We Are Safe

Sacred blessings, miracles and gifts are kept safe.

Have you ever been so terrified that fight-or-flight was not even an option? Have you ever been frozen by fear? Fear that was imposed upon you by another person or the shock of horrific news that cut so deep, every part of you went numb and you collapsed inside yourself and then separated from yourself? If you have never experienced that type of fear, shock and trauma, I am grateful you haven't, and you should be, too. Almost all of youth and young adults I have been blessed to serve have experienced that type of fear, shock and trauma.

It was a little after 2:30 a.m. when I received a call on the crisis phone. I heard the mother of a girl I had been working with say, "Can you please come to the hospital? She needs you. She'll only speak with you and your team, no one else." In the background, I heard the girl screaming hysterically, "Tony! Tony, get here now!"

I drove to the hospital, walked in and found the room where the girl, her family and a rape crisis team were trying to talk with her. The girl was in hysterics from the trauma she endured. She was being combative with the hospital staff. When I walked in the room, she ran to me, hugged me and began crying as her entire being trembled. Clinging to me, she just kept repeating my name as I held her and silently prayed for her, asking the Creator to guide me in what I needed to say and do to be of the most benefit for her. One of the most powerful conversations I've ever had in my work as a Street Outreach Worker happened in that moment, in only two sentences.

I said to the girl, "You don't have to cry because you're safe now."

She answered, "I know I'm safe now, that's why I'm crying."

There was so much wisdom in the girl's one sentence that spoke volumes about relationships and safety. I was able to convince her to tell the rape crisis team everything she could remember and to comply with the rape kit to help law enforcement send the predators to prison. I was only able to convince her to speak with them because of the safety the Creator allowed her to feel in my presence. She felt safe in my presence because wherever I am called, I invite the Creator to be the *Presence* that abounds and surrounds us.

A Street Outreach Worker saw, heard, believed, accepted and had faith in her. How could she not feel safe? It was more than *feeling* safe; it was truth. A Street Outreach Worker, by and with the power of the Creator, makes any place a safe place because of the Creator's presence through us. What the girl learned before the Street Outreach Worker came into her life is that conflict, no matter how miniscule, has one result - violence. Whether the violence was physical, where someone is beaten for having a bad day, a different opinion or saying a little too much; or the type of violence where someone is ostracized, no longer to be included. Then there was perhaps the worst violence of all. The violence of when someone disappears, not away from you, but in front of you; a disappearing act with the pop of a pill, the piercing of a needle, the gulp of some alcohol, a puff of some smoke or a snort of some powder, then the person she knew, just moments before, disappeared, and so did her safety. The Street Outreach Worker would never try to interpret her traumatic experiences but would also never allow those traumatic experiences to interpret her. Although our experiences form us and shape us, they do not have to imprison us. The place and space of safety that came freely in the presence of the Street Outreach Worker freed her. Knowing her life, words, thoughts, good and bad days, mood swings, laughter, prayers, love, tears, hopes, dreams, and fears were safe with the Street Outreach Worker, liberated her from the worst kind of prison - a life sentence, not behind bars, but within her mind. Because a Street Outreach Worker gave her safety, she began to feel safe and take refuge within her own heart.

When We Know We Are Trusted

We trust sacred blessings, miracles and gifts.

The goal of the Street Outreach Worker is to get the youth and young adults we serve to trust themselves. In my experience, there seems to be a pervasive attitude in this world that people cannot change. Yes, people love to root for the underdog. Yes, people love to hear stories of redemption. But when the underdog is someone close to you, a person you know or someone you knew, there seems to be reluctance in rooting for and believing in the power of life-changing transformation. We often miss or dismiss transformation in people we've personally known, but do not know now, because we fail to see the present, beautiful, *new creation* the Creator has miraculously transformed them to be.

For years I worked with a man who had a violent past and served time in prison. When no one else could connect with a young person, especially young people who were gang affiliated, he could. For fifteen years he had done nothing criminal, worked youth programs full-time, was and still is a *new creation* in and with the Creator. Yet, every time he would speak in the community, delivering presentations about youth violence prevention, there were members of the community who would say, "He hasn't changed, because people like him don't change." People do change. People do transform. People do grow back into the likeness and image of the Creator we are all created as, but sometimes walk away from due to pain, loss, tragedy and trauma. Healing happens. Miracles happen. I have witnessed too many miracles to be a skeptic. I have also witnessed too many skeptics who will never see miracles, even when the miracle stands right in front of them. The job of the Street Outreach Worker is to see possibilities where others only see problems. Street Outreach Workers see miracles and trust the sacred process of love and service. Street Outreach Workers trust those they serve. Street Outreach Workers guide those they serve to trust themselves again.

There was a lot of work that went into getting three young men into one of our programs. Many midnight hours and painstaking, street-level interventions, but finally, those young men, all of whom were affiliated with the same gang, agreed to participate in our GED program. Once in the program, they of course participated in other positive activities, and seeds of love and service were offered to them daily.

The three young men were participating and doing well for several weeks. Each of them was given the same attention, love, service and guidance. Each of them seemed to be receiving the love, service and guidance to the best of their abilities. One day, I happened to be in front of the building and all three of the young men came outside. Two of the young men walked straight towards a car with some people in it and got inside the vehicle. The other young man paced back and forth in front of me as someone from inside the car shouted, "Get in, man. Stop acting like a little bit*h!"

The young man who was pacing back and forth, walked up to me, "Tony, I don't know what to do, man." His eyes were welled up with tears of frustration. Remember to never underestimate the power of belonging. This was one of those moments. Something was about to go down. Wherever the young men in the car were going, it was not a good place. I knew it, and most importantly, the young man in front of me, whose frustration was so high he accidentally broke the plastic pen he was holding as he gripped it like it was some type of lifeline, knew it, too. I looked at him and shared, "Life doesn't have to be a closed-book test, young brother. Open your heart and receive the answers. You know what to do. I'm not interfering. I trust you. Right now, you have to trust you."

He paced back and forth as the other young men in the car taunted him. Eventually, the young man threw his broken pen on the ground and walked back inside the building. Once he went inside the building, the car with the other young men drove off. I walked back inside the building and found the young man sitting outside of his GED class. The GED instructor walked out and asked him if he was going to come back to class. I informed the instructor he just passed one of his biggest tests. The GED instructor looked at us curiously and smiled as the young man told her about what happened. I will never forget the young man saying, "Doing the right thing is f**king hard, man. The GED test ain't gonna be sh*t after that test."

All the young man's frustration about the decision he made that day was alleviated the following day. We received word the young men in the car were pulled over by the police on their way to retaliate against a rival gang. The police found illegal firearms in the trunk of the vehicle and all the young men were charged. Eventually, each of them did no less than two years in prison for illegal firearms charges. The Creator guided me not to interfere with the process of trust. The young man knew we trusted him; he needed to learn to trust himself, and the Creator gave him the opportunity, strength and insight for that to happen.

A Street Outreach Worker saw, heard, believed, accepted, had faith in, and brought safety to that young man. How could he not know he was trusted? That young man had given his trust to many who broke his heart. When he agreed to come to our program, he didn't know why he was giving life and trust another chance. In the moment in front of the building where he found himself at a crucial crossroads, he discovered why. He told me, "When you told me you trusted me, it went straight to my soul, man. Trust renewed me and trusting myself in that moment changed my life forever."

When We Know Peace

We give peace to sacred blessings, miracles and gifts.

What is greater than peace? Isn't peace what we truly want for our loved ones and ourselves? All the other things we think we want are just *things*, *circumstances* and *changes* we believe will give us peace. Deep within our souls our beings are moved by

111

and towards peace. We have a longing for the Creator and know the level of which we are experiencing the Creator in our lives by the level of peace we are experiencing.

I had the opportunity to facilitate a gang intervention with a young person. There were many positive seeds planted in the young person's life before that evening, and for that I am grateful. There was also a lot of weeding out of negative seeds that were planted in the young person's life before that evening, and for that I am even more grateful.

When the young person heard me say to her, "You're a sacred blessing, miracle and gift. You are not a gangster; you are a Godster. You're a child of the Creator," she shook and tears welled up in her eyes. She instantly remembered the sacred, and began talking about when and why she stopped believing those truths about herself. After several hours, she made the internal transformation and wanted that to be matched with an external change. She gave me all her gang affiliated items. One item was a rosary she only wore because its color matched that of the gang she was previously affiliated with. In exchange, I gave her a tree of life necklace so she has a symbol to wear that represents healing, growth, beauty and positive transformation. She was also going to get a new rosary, not to wear, but to use to pray and remind her of what she is whenever she is bombarded by the lies of what she isn't.

When she exchanged all her gang affiliated items for a tree of life necklace, she smiled, "I haven't felt like this in a long time."

"Like what?" I inquired.

"I feel light. Things aren't heavy. I feel peace."

In that moment she was being seen as the sacred blessing, miracle and gift she is, so she was willing to see, hear and believe that about herself again. She reclaimed her truth, which will always bring us peace. The truth is not heavy and does not hurt; the lies are heavy and hurt deeply.

Youth and young adults can let their guard down with Street Outreach Workers. They can be themselves and experience the power of being invulnerable by being vulnerable, which is a manifestation of courage that can only occur when someone knows they are safe. A Street Outreach Worker's presence provides peace. Sometimes, youth and young adults who have seldom experienced peace do not know how to respond to peace because they are so accustomed to swimming in chaos. For those who have not experienced much peace, it can be loud, uncomfortable and not easy to digest. Street Outreach Workers, through love, time and consistency give peace to the youth and young adults we serve. Most importantly, the youth and young adults we serve begin to piece peace together, and remember the peace they sought outside of themselves was within them all along.

When We Know Our Life is of Benefit to Others

We know sacred blessings, miracles and gifts are of benefit to others.
What do you do with years filled with heartbreak, loss and trauma? What do you do when trauma hijacks your life with anxiety, panic attacks, addiction and self-sabotage? It seems absurd to tell the youth and young adults who have experienced every form of abuse imaginable and unimaginable that one day their greatest struggles will become the greatest gifts they have to share with others. It's even more absurd for the youth and young adults to hear such a message, until they realize the person delivering it is a living example of the message.

Most Street Outreach Workers have experienced some or all of what those they serve have experienced. This is not always the case, but in my experience, more often than not it is. Many Street Outreach Workers have experienced both the depths of trauma and the heights of transformation and triumph. We are talking about spiritual growth. Why spiritual growth? Because I have never witnessed true transformation and healing occur within myself or anyone else at the cognitive level alone. True healing and transformation happens spiritually. There are steps we take on the cognitive level that get us to our *sacred moment* where healing happens, but cognitive steps, in and of themselves, especially if those steps are not towards the Creator and back to our hearts, will not provide the healing and transformation we need and deserve.

Have you ever known someone who can recite the Bible, yet you have rarely, if ever, witnessed them live it? Whether it is the Bible, other spiritual writings, the twelve steps of Alcoholics Anonymous or Narcotics Anonymous, there are many people who know something intellectually but struggle to live it, or never even attempt to live it. When we know something, it is more than cognitive. It permeates our being and becomes a way of life in public and private. This is who Street Outreach Workers are – living examples of love, hope, faith and charity, who don't just show up, but show the way, because they don't just know *about* the way, they *know* the way.

I received a call from a school about four young men who were affiliated with a gang. The school staff and outside counselors could not reach them, so I was asked to come and meet with the four young men. I agreed, went to the school, and met the young men in a conference room.

When I walked into the conference room the first words out of my mouth were, "Hello, sacred blessings, miracles and gifts." One of the young men leaned over towards his friend and under his breath said, "This mother f**ker." All four of the young men laughed. I laughed, too, and pointed towards myself, "This mother f**ker loves you and wants you to live. I am not going to fight you for your healing. How about the four of you give me two minutes of your undivided attention. And if after what I have to say, you think I'm full of sh*t, just get up and walk out. No questions asked."

Their curiosity was peaked, as one of them asked, "Just two minutes?"

"Just two minutes of your undivided attention. That's all. Nothing more. After the two minutes if you never want to speak with me again, cool."

They agreed to give me the two minutes. In one sweeping, Creator-invoked flow, they heard these words come through me, "All of you have been told time and time again you will be dead or in prison before you are eighteen years old. You have had teachers, counselors and adults talk *at* you, but not *with* you. You've had few, if any adults listen to you. If your childhood pillow could speak, it would tell us about all the nights you cried, screamed and begged the Creator to change your situation. You held on as long as you could through the sounds of glass breaking, gunshots, screams and the sirens of ambulances and police cars. You held on as long as you could through the sights of violence, blood, beatings and cheatings. You held on as long as you

could through disappointments, pain, loss and tragedy. None of you were out in the streets throwing up your set at age six, seven, eight or nine, and if you were, you were only repeating behavior you saw. You sure as hell weren't trying to be hard on Saturday morning while you watched cartoons and ate Captain Crunch cereal. You were all children who had been disappointed and hurt, but despite that happening repeatedly, you swore you'd never be like what you witnessed others doing. What you really wanted was time with those who didn't give it to you, comfort from those you didn't get it from, and security from those who were supposed to protect you but left you or hurt you. There was a void so deep in your life, and all your prayers never seemed to be answered, so one day at the age of twelve or thirteen you said *f**k it*. Clinging to those two magic words when the pain became too great, your heart shattered, and you just got tired of hanging on. You walked away from your heart and into gang life, not because you're bad, but because you were hurt. Now, if you ever want to work with me and visit those wounded boys inside you to heal the present young men you are, I am available. It will be challenging. There will be ups, downs, setbacks and disappointments. However, on the other side of that seventeen-inch walk from our heads back to our hearts, there is a healing and peace that's indescribable. After you walk that journey, you will be warriors for and with the

Creator. Shining lights for others who need to hear from someone who has been there and lived it. I don't give a sh*t if you're not afraid to die. My concern is you are afraid to live. Live with me, brothers! All your struggles hold the key to your greatness and the key to heal others. You are a great benefit to this world and to me. Live with me, brothers!"

Their eyes were wide. Their hearts open. The leader shook his head in both relief and disbelief, "That was some real sh*t."

I went well over two minutes, but they didn't know that because they were all in, and stayed all in. They went on to participate in our program and made the slow but sure changes on deep levels. When the school staff asked me how I was able to reach them, I told them the truth. I told them Spirit reached them, because youth work, real youth work, is Spirit-led.

A Street Outreach Worker teaches, not just by words but by example, that any poison can be transformed into a healing medicine. Street Outreach Workers offer the ingredients of love, faith, hope and compassion. Those sacred ingredients mix with anger, false pride, un-forgiveness, hurt, pain and loss, until the youth or young adult awakens from a trauma-filled coma as a healed, renewed creation, with many tests that transform into testimonies. It is an experience no one can take from you. It comes with a powerful love and gratitude that awakens you, and makes you want to give all the healing and transformation you've received to others, so others awaken from nightmares that need not be. Street Outreach Workers show youth and young adults their lives are of benefit to others, then the youth and young adults begin to live to be of benefit to others. This is how the torch of street outreach, love, service and leadership passes from one generation to the next.

When We Know We Are Loved

We love sacred blessings, miracles and gifts because they reflect the truth of the Great Love that created us exactly like Itself.

I agree with the statement from the book *A Course in Miracles*, *everything is either an expression of love or a call for love*. If we contemplate the behavior of others, or most importantly, the behavior of ourselves, we can see everything we do is expressing love or calling for love. We have all called out for love in a variety of ways. Sometimes we have called out for love in direct, coherent ways. Other times we have called out for love in emotional outbursts that stemmed from pain. Sometimes we are not even aware we are calling out for love. It is impossible to crave something we have never tasted. As human beings, love is perhaps the only thing we crave even if we have never experienced it from other people. We have a craving for love because we *are* love. Love comes from within us because it *is* us. If we don't deny ourselves the love we are, our cravings for love will always be quenched.

I was facilitating a group at a facility for survivors of sex trafficking. We were talking about substance abuse when the Creator threw me a curveball. I stopped and told the girls, "Okay, the Creator just threw me a curveball, and what I am about to say may not be on topic with what we are talking about, but since the Creator is telling me to say this, I know it's for someone here, or maybe everyone here." I took a deep breath and shared, "Has anyone here ever been in a relationship where you saw all of the greatness within a person, but that person could not see it within themselves?" All the girls raised their hands and exclaimed, "Yes!" I continued, "At one point or another we have all done that to a greater or lesser extent. Now, how many of you have been in a relationship where you desperately tried to get the person you were in a relationship with to see what you saw in them? And you were so certain about their ability to be the wonderful, loving, caring person you saw, but no matter how many times you tried to get them to see what you saw in them, you were talked down to or abused?" Before I even finished asking that question most of the girls had tears flowing down their faces because they all had that experience. After I checked in with the girls and made sure they were okay to continue, I concluded, "Finding yourself in that predicament doesn't make you weak. Remember we are here to rise with love because love is light! We have been through enough condemnation, and condemnation is not of the Creator. The lesson is simple: *we cannot have a relationship with someone else's potential.* The only person's potential we can have a relationship with is our own potential. The only relationship we can have with others is with who they are choosing to be right now. We do not need to subject ourselves to any form of abuse, enduring years and tears of desperation, waiting for someone else to become the greatness we see in them, because that person may never choose to live their sacred potential. Besides, all the greatness we see in others wouldn't be visible to us if that same greatness wasn't within us. See the Creator's greatness within you and develop the best possible relationship with the Creator and yourself."

Almost all the girls shared stories about how much hurt they experienced while trying to have a relationship with someone's potential. They all shared the curveball the Creator gave me was exactly what they needed to hear. Sharing what the Creator gives us to share, even when we don't know why, is a sure way to have and share peace.

After that group, one of the girls, a new placement at the facility who had just been rescued from a trafficker, was standing in front of me along with one of the staff members. With a combination of tears and smiles, she looked as if she wanted to say something to me. "Are you okay?" I asked her. She nodded her head, "Yes. I just want you to know when you told us we cannot have a relationship with someone else's potential, that really spoke to me. It spoke to all of us. Thank you."

I beamed, "Thank you. You are a sacred blessing, miracle and gift. There is something else I want you to know. I love you. I don't want you. I don't want anything from you. All I want is for you to remember, know, and live the greatness the Creator has created you as." She smiled, gave me a hug, then walked back to another part of the facility with the staff member who accompanied her. A few days later the clinical director of the facility informed me the girl shared with their staff that I was the first man who ever told her she is a sacred blessing, miracle and gift. And I was the first man who has ever told her that he loves her, and she knew there were no strings attached and no negative motive. She shared that knowing she is loved unconditionally gave her a peace she had never felt before.

When the sacred words *I love you* are pure, something miraculous happens. Conversations become sacred communion, where love is invoked and leads the way. Every time a Street Outreach Worker sees, hears, believes, accepts, has faith in, makes a safe place for, trusts, gives peace to, and reminds youth and young adults their lives are beneficial to others and this world, the thick walls that lock away their beautiful hearts crumble. Those walls are flushed out through the river of their sacred, cleansing tears, and they know love again. Most importantly, they reconnect with the love of the Creator, and walk back to the love they are – the love they've always been.

You Are a Lion

I was called to a scene where a young man was supposedly just having a bad day and was in a parking lot at an apartment complex experiencing some stress. What I wasn't told over the phone, because the person who called me didn't know, was the young man was homicidal and suicidal and had a handgun in his front waistband. I never met him before. There were seconds for me to establish a connection. I sat on a curb about ten feet away from him and informed him I'm not law enforcement, but some people who truly care about him called me to see if I can be of service to him. He said nothing. He was just looking at me, but more looking through me with a thousand-yard stare.

The young man had a distinct look. He had dreadlocks that were tinted on the ends and was wearing a Bob Marley t-shirt. He had several tattoos of lions on his arms. As I sat there looking away from him but watching him closely out of my peripheral, I had no idea what he was going to do. My phone was in my pocket, and I knew it would not be a good move at that moment to reach for it and dial 911. Once again, the Creator had placed me on the razor's edge, and it was the Creator Who needed to come through and do this. I silently said a prayer and was immediately guided by the Creator with what to say.

"You're a lion!" I exclaimed, as I calmly stood up.

He looked at me and cautiously asked, "What made you say that?"

"Your hair for one. One of Bob Marley's songs is *Iron Lion Zion*. Those dreadlocks you have are strong roots. I've heard some Rastafarians talk about dreadlocks. They would say dreadlocks are the crown from Jah, the Creator, the Most High. Those who are in this world doing evil know the power of those dreadlocks, so they feel dread when they see a lion like you come through as a power of good and righteousness. You're a protector and provider, placed here to help and protect the weak. You are a lion!"

His eyes softened a bit as the thousand-yard stare subsided, when he shared, "I didn't know all that about Bob Marley, dreadlocks or lions. I like Bob Marley and lions."

"Yeah, man. You should research Bob some more. There's a whole lot more to Bob and Rastafarians than the herb they use as a sacrament," I shared with a smile.

The young man smiled and shook his head in agreement. I left a pause for him to fill it in with whatever was on his mind, but he didn't speak, so I continued, "You know lions, even as powerful as they are, still get wounded and need time to heal. Even the strongest of lions don't try to make it alone, which is why they have prides and take care of each other. You are most definitely a lion. You are strong, handsome, intelligent, courageous and kind. Someone from your pack called me and let me know you're hurting. They didn't call me because they think you're weak; they called me because you are hurting and wandered away from the pride. They don't want you to get lost out in the wilderness because no lion, no matter how strong, can survive on their own. Lions are smart like that, you know?"

He stood there completely mesmerized with tears in his eyes. I knew the Creator had him. I just looked off in the distance and let whatever was going on between the young man and the Creator run its course. After a few minutes, the young man began to talk about all the pressures of living a positive life and how easy it is to get pulled back into what he worked hard to get away from. He shared that he did pull the gun on his brother a little while before I got there and came outside to shoot himself right where we were standing. The more he talked, the more pain he revealed about his past and his fears about his future. I stood with him, listening to him so intensely I was sweating.

After the young man finished talking, his shoulders were relaxed and his hand was not on the gun. The miracle happened, so the rest was simply follow through. The young man gave the gun to his brother who lived in the apartment above where we were standing, packed some of his clothes, and allowed me to take him to an emergency psychiatric treatment center that he and I jokingly referred to as his temporary lion's den of healing.

Love Keeps Us Calm in a Barrage of Bullets

It was my turn to pick up the youth who were participants in our after-school program. My coworker and I had a van full of teenagers when we arrived at the last high school on our route. We were picking up the last two youth before going back to the facility. When we pulled up next to the high school, fights began breaking out all around us and all over the front of the school. There were even some adults fighting with students. My coworker and I were not going to allow the two youth we were picking up to try to maneuver through the mayhem alone. He saw the two young people standing startled by the front door of the school. We agreed my coworker would go get them, walk them to our van, and I would stand outside of the van, just outside the driver's door with the window down, keeping any violence away from our youth, while keeping our youth calm by speaking with them and reassuring them we are safe.

I was outside of the van doing my best to keep our youth's attention on me by talking with them and telling them some short stories. There was a car with several people in it, parked directly across the street from us, right behind where I was standing. A vehicle sped towards us from up the street, slammed its brakes and stopped right behind me. I pushed my body against our van because I thought the car was going to hit me. I never stopped looking our youth directly in their eyes and continued sharing some humorous short stories, which soothed them and may have hid my apprehension about what was happening. The driver of the car behind me got out with an AK-47 assault rifle, walked around his car, and unloaded a full magazine into the vehicle parked with several people in it. For a moment, I thought about intervening in the shooting when the Creator steadied me in my calling at that time. My calling was to protect and comfort the van full of youth we were responsible for. Even with as loud as the gunfire from that weapon was, I never broke eye contact with the youth in our van, and never hesitated in saying all the words the Creator gave me to share with them at that moment. My coworker returned to the van with the two youth we were picking up. We all jumped in the van and sped away.

We went to the facility where we circled up and processed, not just what had happened in front of the school, but all the trauma the youth we serve have endured in their young lives, because moments like that bring back many memories. The remaining part of the talking circle that day was led by the older youth. They wanted to transform something negative into something positive, and began plans for a community peace building project which they eventually implemented.

We found out from a local police officer that everyone inside the vehicle that was shot up survived but were all severely injured. There was no bravado in my thought process or actions that day, only love. If there's such a thing as courage, I think we can only find it in love. If my last moments on this beautiful Earth was looking into the eyes of the youth we were responsible to care for while making them laugh and reassuring them they are safe, I fulfilled my calling. For years I did my best to show them how to live, so if in that moment, the time had come to show them how to pass on from this life, the lesson would have been to pass on from this life *on* your path, never *off* your path.

A Few Miles Further Than the Extra Mile

On New Year's Eve of 2014 while most people were in the comfort of their own homes visiting with family and friends, our street outreach team was transporting a young person who was left stranded in front of the Salvation Army.

When no one else was available to assist the fourteen-year-old girl, we did. We contacted the girl's mother, CPS, police department and Department of Public Safety to confirm the youth was who she said she was and that we were not transporting her back to predators. After coordinating with the youth's mother, law enforcement, and obtaining the proper documents from the youth's mother, we transported the girl four hundred and ten miles.

Our street outreach team departed with the young lady from the Salvation Army at approximately 4:30 p.m., purchased snacks for the trip and proceeded to drive. Initially, the team had arranged to meet with the mother and family at a halfway point, but unfortunately, an ice storm that hit Texas that night forced the family to take shelter only about two hours from their hometown. Our team prayed, had a conversation and quickly decided to go the distance.

At approximately 9 p.m., there were cars and 18-wheelers off the road in every direction. Driving speeds reduced from sixty-five miles per hour to twenty miles or less per hour. The windshield wipers froze, and because of this, the wipers began leaving black streaks on the windshield making it necessary to pull over every fifty miles to clean the windshield.

Our street outreach team arrived at 2:30 a.m. reuniting the girl with her mother and younger brother. The team visited with the family for a moment then began the return trip, safely returning home the next day, New Year's Day, at approximately 12:00 noon. Our street outreach team ended 2014 and began 2015 in the same manner we operate on a daily and nightly basis within the community - by going a few miles further than the extra mile.

The Creator Doesn't Choose the Qualified, the Creator Qualifies the Chosen

Around midnight I received a call from an investigator. I woke up, answered the phone and heard the investigator say, "Anthony, I have Rome on the other line and I need to know something." Half asleep, I asked, "Who's Rome?"

"Rome, Italy. I have law enforcement from Rome, Italy on the line and they found a girl who they believe is a survivor of human trafficking. The girl is not speaking to them. They want to know how to get a traumatized child to talk."

My first thought was, *I'm not a world-renowned expert in trauma. There are experts who are renowned in the field of trauma who could and should be called for matters such as this.* That thought was quickly interrupted by the investigator, "Anthony! How do they do it?" I told the investigator to call me back in five minutes. When the investigator asked me why they needed to call me back in five minutes, I told the investigator I needed to pray. I hung up the phone and prayed. The Creator gave me the answer. Right at about the five-minute mark, the investigator called me back. I told the investigator to tell law enforcement in Rome to have the lead person who is attempting to communicate with the girl to sit on the floor to her left. Place a blanket on her if they haven't already, bring her cookies, popcorn, pizza, cotton candy, a cute stuffed animal to hold, and then just sit with her in peace, not as an overwhelming, law enforcement presence. The investigator, with no hesitation said, "Okay. I will relay the message and call you back when I hear something."

About an hour later the investigator called me back, "Well, it worked. Thank you so much for sharing that information. How did you know what needed to be done?" I reminded the investigator I did not know what needed to be done. That is why I prayed and asked the Creator what needed to be done. I also reminded the investigator to thank the Creator, not me.

I don't think people know how serious I am when I say *the Creator doesn't choose the qualified, the Creator qualifies the chosen.*

I have no credentials, yet I have been placed in positions that normally require no less than a master's degree, and even some positions that required a PhD. When we follow our calling, doors will open when our minds and hearts are in alignment with the Creator to be a vessel of love and service to others. What can happen naturally is nothing compared to what can happen supernaturally, when we allow the Creator to do through us what we could never do alone.

On another occasion, I was finishing some paperwork in my office at our emergency shelter when one of my coworkers asked me to assist with an intervention. One of the youth at our shelter was having a difficult moment. He was fourteen years old and diagnosed with multiple personality disorder – thirteen different personalities. He had been working with psychiatrists for several years but made little progress. I went to the room where the boy and my coworker were sitting. He kept talking about the torment of the thirteen different personalities and was terrified they would control him forever. I asked him, "Do you want them gone?"

"Yes," he answered.

I went back to my office, got some markers, a poster board and tape. I said a prayer asking the Creator to guide and provide, then went back to the room where the boy and my coworker awaited my return. I placed the poster board on the wall and had him tell me the names of the thirteen personalities. I listed the names in the order he gave them. I asked him to describe each one of them. I listed their attributes next to their names, and it was soon revealed the attributes each personality has were all necessary attributes that brought him courage, comfort, relief, rest, security, peace, and got him through some life-or-death situations. He recognized that and said it aloud before I pointed it out to him.

In a little over an hour he was able to process that he doesn't have different personalities controlling him, but the attributes of each of the personalities are all traits he needed to survive. Next, we looked at what attributes were serving him and making his life better as well as the attributes that were hindering him. He did most of the talking, and as we concluded the intervention, he asked, "Did we just reintegrate my personalities?"

I smiled, "The Creator did. You are a sacred blessing, miracle and gift."

The boy never again brought up the personalities by name but began recognizing his emotions and thought process more clearly, so he was able to use coping skills with more success because he was once again in control. He felt good and empowered about the progress.

About a week later his therapist came to visit him and have a session. After their session his therapist wanted to meet with me. In their session he told his therapist about his thirteen personalities being reintegrated and how good he felt. She wanted to know exactly what occurred during the intervention I facilitated, so I walked her through it step-by-step. After I explained what happened I told her he is happy, more peaceful and empowered, so she could use that as a building block to continue his progress. But the only thing his therapist was focused on was my lack of credentials. I assured her I was not trying to overstep my boundaries, and I was only providing an intervention because initially he was having thoughts about harming himself. During the conversation with the therapist it became apparent she was much more focused on credentials than the progress the boy had made. The therapist said to me, "You're not qualified to do what you did."

I responded, "You can't get more qualified than actually being able to do it." She didn't say another word. She just shook her head and walked out of my office.

Always remember Who has called you so you never forget Who to call upon to guide you. Yes, read, study, complete a degree, or several degrees, attend as much training and workshops as you can, but always allow the Creator to filter and guide the information you are being given, so what you retain and share is of true benefit to others. Even when you are dealing with a situation that is so-called textbook, don't presume you know. Double check with the Creator and invite the Creator into every situation to guide and bless the outcome for those you are serving, because things are not always what they seem.

It's not Always What it Seems

A counselor called me and asked if I'd be willing to facilitate a homelessness prevention meeting with a sixteen-year-old young man and his family. The young man's parents did not want him at home anymore due to him being defiant and disrespectful to his parents and grandparents. I drove to the residence, knocked on the door and was welcomed inside the home. I sat down at the kitchen table with the young man's mother, grandmother and grandfather. The young man was upstairs in his room. The family explained they heard about our shelter and wanted me to take him because they wanted him out of the house. The family told me about all the bad things the young man had been doing. Things like not listening, arguing, yelling and slamming doors. I understand those behaviors are not conducive for a peaceful household, and healthy boundaries need to be set, but there was obviously much more going on, and the Creator quickly revealed what it was.

After listening to the complaints about the young man from his family, I asked if one of them would please go and see if he's willing to speak with me. The grandfather went upstairs, and after several minutes he and the young man came downstairs. I asked the young man if he would be willing to speak with me. He shook his head yes. Then I asked his mom if it would be okay if the young man and I went outside on their front porch to talk in private. His mother had no problem with that, so the young man and I walked outside onto the porch and sat down.

The young man and I sat in silence for a while. After about five minutes, I told him, "I am not your expert. You are your expert. I can only be an expert of my experience. There is one thing I know, and that is you are a sacred blessing, miracle and gift." As has happened so many times before, hearing his truth, perhaps for the first time in a long time, did not cause him to think, it caused him to feel. There is a difference between speaking to someone's brain and speaking to someone's heart. He knew his heart was being spoken to. He began to sob uncontrollably, paced around the front yard of his home for a bit, then walked back onto the porch and asked if he could share something with me away from the porch, in the front yard, because he didn't want to risk his family hearing him. I said, "Of course." We walked off of the porch and onto the front yard where he leaned up against a tree and cried some more. As he cried, I reminded him how courageous he is to cry, and that real men cry. He was reminded his tears are not weak, but strong and courageous. He took a deep breath and shared, "I'm going to kill myself tonight. I am going to use my belt to hang myself. That's what I am going to do."

After the young man said those words, within my own mind, I looked up at the Creator, and silently said, "Just a homelessness prevention call, huh?" I sat down on the Earth and asked the young man to sit down for a moment with me. He sat down in front of me. Praying through it, I asked him, "I know you don't want to end your life. You want to end whatever pain you're feeling, right?" He began to cry even more, as he answered, "Yes."

"What is the pain you are trying to end?"

"Lifelong pain," he answered. "My dad isn't around, and I miss him. My family only sees the bad things I do, never the good. My girlfriend is the only one who understands me and if I did choose to stay alive it would be for her, nobody else."

I asked him, "Have you ever been in a crowd and felt so alone it literally made you feel cold to the point where cold shivers surged throughout your body?"

The young man looked at me confused and surprised, "Yes. How did you know that?"

"Because I have felt the same way on more than one occasion. Moments in my life have been difficult. Some more than others. There have been moments in my life when nothing external could bring comfort, peace and warmth to me. I felt alone, even in a crowd. It takes courage, but I reached out for help. After all you've been through, and you've been through a lot, what have you held onto?"

"That something will change. I believe at some point in the future things will change for the better."

"Some point in the future has to be met by you. Maybe that some point in the future is right now. Maybe, just maybe, the Creator guided us together right now for you to hear this: There was a young man who wanted to kill himself, but he allowed help to enter his life. That young man felt broken, betrayed, lost, scared and alone. That young man tried to numb his pain with drugs, alcohol, excitement and whatever worked to temporarily make him forget about what he was running from. Then, one day, all bets were off when the numbing agents wore off, and the only thing he could see was his death. Not because he wanted to end his life, but because he wanted to end his pain. The Creator sent that young man an older man to come into his life and remind him of the sacred blessing, miracle and gift he is. Now, many years later, that young man is an older man, sitting right here in front of a young man, as living proof this moment in your life is challenging, but this moment in your life is a *moment* in your life, not the *rest* of your life."

I couldn't hold back my tears and why would I? I would never disrespect someone I am serving by wanting them to open their heart while keeping mine closed. My tears ran down my face incessantly as the Creator continued to guide my words, "Now we sit here, at your crossroads for you to live or take your own life. Whatever you choose, remember you didn't create yourself, so you cannot kill yourself. However, the One Who created you can fill the void you've had for so long. You will always know when the Creator is speaking to you directly because you will feel good and are reminded that you are a sacred blessing, miracle and gift."

The young man began sobbing again and fell into my arms. How important are tears? Sometimes when someone has the courage to cry it will save their life. He decided to get further help. He decided to live.

I explained to him I am a mandated reporter and I must tell his family what is happening with him. I told him we can go inside together, he can tell them and I will be there for support; or I can tell them while he sits with us. He wanted me to tell his family. We went back inside the house, sat down at the table with his family and I explained what was happening with the young man. The family immediately went from angry and ready to kick him out of their lives to compassionate, loving and supportive, embracing him with care and encouragement. As the family wrapped their love around him, they were all crying and hugging each other. While the family was embraced I called an adolescence psychiatric treatment center, explained the situation, and they held a bed for the young man. The family helped the young man pack some of his clothes, then they all went together to help the young man take his first steps on his journey of hope and healing.

Behind the Door

I got a call from a residential program about a girl who wanted out of a lifestyle that was of benefit only to the predators selling her. The girl was residing with predators in an apartment complex that was controlled by a gang. The residential program staff didn't have the experience to go to where the girl was. They were afraid to go, as most people would be. I immediately attempted to route some assistance for the intervention. My street outreach partner was on the other side of town dealing with a different crisis call. My usual police contacts were on various scenes of their own, and I knew I had to get there fast. I drove by myself to an apartment complex that even the police will not enter without backup. Nevertheless, I had backup. I always do. We all do when we remember to invite the Creator.

As I drove past the lookouts at the entrance of the apartment building and entered the parking lot, there were many people keeping a steady eye on me. I said a prayer. Got out of my vehicle and walked up the stairs to the second floor of the apartments, turned right, and two doors down on my left-hand side was the apartment the girl was in. The apartment door was shut, so I walked up and knocked on the door. The door opened. I could see many men, some young and some older, all wearing the same color shirt, which happened to be the color that represents the gang that controls those apartments. I let them know I was there for the girl and said her name. A man motioned for me to come inside. Again, I entered with the Creator, so I was not alone. I walked down the hallway and saw the girl packing her suitcase. She said she didn't need any help packing and finished placing all her belongings in the suitcase. I carried her suitcase down the hall and out the door of that apartment. As we exited the apartment and walked towards my vehicle, there were many condescending remarks being said to the girl and me. I placed her suitcase in the trunk of my car, then we both got in my car and I transported her to the residential program that was expecting her. The girl didn't have the means, nor the support to get to the residential program by herself. She was isolated and made to believe that even if she reached out for help, no one would help her. The Creator proved the predators wrong and I am honored I was chosen in that moment for that purpose.

Did I feel fear? Of course. I knew where I was. I have witnessed enough, more than enough on the streets to know, not only all that could happen, but how quick it does happen. What was most important in that moment was the girl, not my fear. What that girl had endured behind that door was nothing compared to any emotions I felt outside of that door. The Creator delivered her to victory, and for that I am grateful.

Never Try to Talk Someone Out of Their Faith

Most of my experience has been serving youth and young adults. However, there were a few years when I served adults. I had a caseload that fluctuated between eighty-four and over one hundred people who were all diagnosed with paranoid schizophrenia. My calling at that time was to find them, get them to and from their doctor's appointments, and support them in various life skills so they could live their best life possible.

One day I was looking for a man who was in his late sixties. He had an apartment but was never there. He struggled with addiction to crack cocaine. Because of the combination of his addiction, living on the streets and lifelong trauma, he was taken advantage of many times. He was often assaulted and robbed. He was a small man with a humungous spirit and beautiful heart. When I was making my rounds throughout several areas, I saw him in an alley sitting beside a dumpster. I parked my vehicle, got out of the car and walked up to him. Glistening with a smile from ear to ear, he exclaimed, "Mr. Tony, it's so good to see you." The joy that man carried within him, despite all he endured throughout his life is something that will always amaze me.

We talked for a while. As usual, he told me he was doing fine, but just cannot get used to living in an apartment and is more comfortable on the streets. He shared that he does go to the apartment to eat when he is hungry. In the middle of our conversation he lifted his shirt up and showed me a huge growth, the size of a softball, which was protruding from the lower, left side of his abdomen. Then he lifted up his right pant leg and showed me an equally large protruding growth on his upper calf. I pleaded with him for well over an hour to allow me to take him to the doctor so medical professionals could check him. No matter what angle I came at him with, he simply said, "God will heal me, Mr. Tony."

I shared with him that I believe in miracles, too, but sometimes the Creator works through others to deliver miracles or deliver us to the miracles. No matter what I said he refused to allow me to take him to get medical attention. I cannot force someone to get medical help. He had my cell phone number, so if he changed his mind he knew he could call me and I would transport him to the doctor's office or

143

hospital. Before I left he wanted to pray with me. I knelt in the alley next to the dumpster with him. We held hands and he shared, "Let's look up, Mr. Tony, then close our eyes and look within. Because God still speaks to us, and people who listen to God are rarely listened to by people who only talk about God." After he said those words, we prayed, and I went back to the office to write my case notes for the day. I felt like I failed because I couldn't convince him to get medical attention. It would be several hours later when I realized I did fail, but not at what I thought.

Later that night I fell asleep on the couch while watching television. In the middle of the night I woke up crying. I sat up knowing I was crying but didn't know why. Then I heard a voice, or better yet, *The* Voice, saying, "Don't ever try to talk any of my children out of their faith again. Do you think my son has survived all these years through all the abuse he endured as a child, teenager, adult, and now middle-aged man because of prescriptions, systems and social services? The only certainty he has ever had is Me, and it is Me he is certain of."

A few weeks later I saw him. He lifted his shirt and showed me the growth was gone. He lifted his pant leg and showed me the other growth was gone, too. He smiled, "I told you God would heal me, Mr. Tony."

What Would He Say to You?

I was driving to facilitate a gang intervention group. That group was a large group and extremely challenging because there were a couple of high-ranking members of rival gangs in the group. On the drive to the group I was praying, asking the Creator to guide me with the message the youth needed to hear. Immediately, I heard the answer spoken to me in my heart, "Ask them what they think Jesus Christ would say to them if He walked into the room."

I arrived at the group and the youth began entering the room and taking their seats. We circled up, and before I asked the question, I asked, "How many of you believe in a Higher Power?" They all raised their hands. Then I asked, "How many of you know your Higher Power as God in terms of Christianity?" They all raised their hands. I had to ask one more thing because I am always conscious to be inclusive and never want to exclude anyone. In some groups, there are many different spiritual beliefs and my calling is not to impose spiritual beliefs, but to work with others to strengthen their own spiritual beliefs in love. I asked, "Just for clarity, everyone here believes in Jesus Christ?" They all answered yes. It was time for me to ask what I was told to ask, "If Jesus Christ walked into this room right now, what would He say to you?"

To my surprise there was no hesitation. One by one, even those who never spoke in group before, began to say things like, "He would say I'm bad." "He would say I'm a sinner." "He would tell me I'm going to hell." The group looked like they were in complete agreement about what Jesus Christ would say to them if He walked into the room, until one of the high-ranking members of a gang shared, "He wouldn't say any of that sh*t to any of us. He would tell us the same thing He's been telling us our entire lives, but some of us have just been too stubborn to listen. He'd tell us He loves us, we're forgiven and to follow Him." As he concluded his statement, I saw him glance across the circle at a rival gang member who was shaking his head in agreement, and shared, "That's real talk. You're right."

The rest of the group that day was led by two high-ranking members of rival gangs, helping everyone in the room, myself included, understand that unlike all the people who've betrayed, hurt and abandoned us, Jesus Christ loves us unconditionally and just wants us to follow Him.

Kids with Parent Problems

It is not uncommon for Street Outreach Workers to get calls from schools, juvenile detention facilities and parents requesting us to come in and make progress with youth and young adults no one else could. There have been times when

146

a youth or young adult chooses to be defiant and disrespectful for no reason other than they felt like it, but those cases are far and few between. In my experience, when a parent brings their kid to me thinking they are a parent with a kid problem, after a little bit of work with the youth and family, the opposite is revealed. The situation is usually a kid with a parent problem. For example, there have been times when a parent brings their child to me and informs me their child came out to them as gay, and the parents tell me their child is having an identity crisis. However, it is really the parents who are having a crisis about their child's identity. I have worked with many youth and young adults living on the streets who are LGBTQ. They found the courage to share with their parents who they truly are, thinking they would be loved and supported, but they were disrespected and rejected. That is one of many reasons why facilitating homelessness prevention in the form of family mediations are crucial moments.

Over my career I have facilitated many family mediations. One thing that's been consistent with families in distress is they are stuck in a cycle of blame. Everyone is trying to figure out who is at the greatest fault, which of course leads to no progress whatsoever. It maintains a cycle of resentment, anger and hurt. Breaking the pattern of the blame cycle must come first. Before diving into the work with a family, I remind them that facing the truth has nothing to do with blame. I have searched for and found truth in many places, but I have never found truth in blame. To assist in breaking the cycle of blame I like to take the family through three questions from Naikan therapy.

Naikan is a Japanese word that translates to *inside looking,* introspection. Naikan therapy was developed in Japan by Yoshimoto Ishin (1916-1988), a businessperson and devout Buddhist. I would encourage you to research the life of Yoshimoto Ishin and Naikan therapy to apply its benefits to your personal life as well as the lives of those you serve. What initially intrigued me about Naikan therapy is that Yoshimoto first introduced it to young people who had been incarcerated. I know from my many years of experience in gang intervention that until a compassionate, loving communication tool is introduced, the blame cycles, whether they are internal or external, keep someone on a continued path of internal and external destruction.

The three questions in Naikan therapy are: What have I received from (person)? What have I given to (person)? What troubles or difficulties have I caused (person)? When facilitated with love, this simple exercise creates a beautiful space of compassion and introspection that, if the family is willing, breaks the blame cycle so the groundwork for healing is created. Think of it like tilling the soil before planting the seeds. The participants are guided to focus on what positive things their family has given them, what positive things they have given their family, and what troubles they have given their family. Almost every time when I facilitate the Naikan questions, no matter how upset the family is, the entire family usually agrees about all the good things they have received from and given to each another. We all fall into negative cycles that require some small shift in perception to awaken us to the many things that are right, especially in moments when all we can see is what's wrong. Participants are not asked to speak about what troubles members of their family have given to them because that is where the blame cycle lies. That does not mean family members are not held accountable. When facilitated correctly, the three Naikan questions bring about individual accountability and individual gratitude, so personal accountability and gratitude organically flows back into the discussions, perceptions and dynamics.

After the first step of Naikan therapy is facilitated, there are steps that follow, such as writing a family vision and mission statement, visits with a family therapist, and further mediations as needed. As a Street Outreach Worker, I often get calls to mediate with families when parents are at their wits' end and ready to throw their child out onto the streets instead of looking within themselves and upwards to the Creator. Throwing your child out onto the streets is not a solution, although there are far too many youth and young adults who've had parents that thought it was. I wrote a letter to parents who threw their children out onto the streets. I met with a young man for breakfast who had been living on the streets for years. His parents threw him out onto the streets. He read the letter I wrote and said I should make the letter public.

Dear Parents Who Threw Their Children Out onto the Streets

Dear Parents Who Threw Their Children Out onto the Streets,

Early this morning at sunrise I saw your son. He emerged from behind a store where he has been sleeping on the concrete. He was trembling from the morning cold, hungry and exhausted. He does not sleep well outside, but he does it every night. I took him to a restaurant where he warmed up from the cold as we ate breakfast together. He is a good young man who is so very talented. He is an amazing artist with a wonderful sense of humor. I thought you might want to know that despite the beatings he suffered within your home and you throwing him out onto the streets, day by day, he's inching his way back to his heart and learning to accept himself as the sacred blessing, miracle and gift he is.

I met your daughter the other night. It was late when the police called my phone and woke me up around 1:00 am. I could hear your daughter screaming in the background as the police officer asked me to come out and see if I could help calm her and get her to a shelter. You see, predators who call themselves pimps manipulated your daughter. Over a period of several months those predators drugged her, violated her and convinced her they care about her. They repeatedly sold her. When I arrived on the scene I looked at your daughter and the first thing I said to her was, "You're a sacred blessing, miracle and gift." I just sat there with her as she was wrapped in a blanket shivering from trauma. The officers also wrapped her in love as we continually reminded her she's safe and none of what happened to her was her fault. As I drove her to a shelter she decided to tell me part of her story. She told me about when she was sexually abused at an early age and held it in for as long as she could. Then one day, with all the courage she could muster, she came to you and told you about what was done to her. To her heartbreaking surprise, you did not believe her. And not only did you not believe her, you demanded she not say anything to anyone. Not long after you didn't believe her, and she stuffed the horrific truth of what happened to her down into the depths of her being as you demanded she do, she began cutting herself, using drugs and drinking alcohol. She told me about all the times you

151

insisted she's crazy and took her to and from psychiatric hospitals telling psychiatrists, psychologists and therapists, "I just don't know what's wrong with my daughter. We've done all we could and there's nothing more we can do for her." The day came when you put some of her belongings in garbage bags, placed them on the porch of your home, and told her, "You just need to leave. We can't handle you anymore." With tears in her eyes, she begged you to listen to her, but you closed the door of your home to your daughter, as the predator who violated her, the one you told her to protect by remaining silent, stood behind you smiling. But don't you worry, despite you not believing her and telling her to suppress the truth, and then numbing the pain of what happened to her by cutting herself, using drugs and alcohol, she's safe now. Now, she is in a place where she's surrounded by people who see her worth, because they treat her like the sacred blessing, miracle and gift she is.

I looked for your son the other day in an abandoned building someone told me he was living in. Some other young people living in the abandoned building told me he took off a few days earlier and they hadn't seen him since. I looked all over the place for him but couldn't find him. I made some missing person flyers and posted them around. He has my number and I hope he calls me to let me know he is safe. Before he went missing, I met him and talked with him many times in a park where he was living. We even had a surprise birthday party for him at the park. He talked about some of the birthdays he remembered having with you. He said the last one was when he was twelve years old. He shed some tears but was extremely grateful to have a birthday celebration with cake, ice cream and a birthday song. He got a new pair of pants and a shirt. He put the new shirt on right away, and as he did, he told me to look at his back. The gashes in his back from when you beat him have healed but the scars are deep, like the wounds you left upon his heart. Of course the police and CPS got involved, but because of your connections nothing ever happened, other than you kicking him out onto the streets because you have a business and a reputation to uphold. I reminded him it is possible for us to count our scars as the number of times we have been healed, not wounded, but I'm not sure when he'll be able to do that. Don't worry, we'll keep looking for him, and when we find him, we'll continue to provide all the love and support he allows us to give.

I went to your daughter's high school graduation. You weren't there, even though she sent you an invitation. A few years ago you remarried and have a new wife who your daughter accepted, respected and adored. But your new wife doesn't like your daughter and didn't want her around. Eventually, your wife told you that you had to choose between your daughter, her and her biological children. You chose your wife and her biological children over your daughter, threw your daughter and her belongings outside and locked the door. Not too long after that is when I met your daughter. I got a call about an amazing senior in high school, who, even though she was homeless, didn't miss a day of school and continued to make all A's and B's. I helped her find a safe place to live, get a job and provided food, clothes and support as she needed. Man, she's smart. She just started her second year of college and is in the process of becoming a counselor to help young people. She says her dream of becoming a counselor is because she knows from her own experience how important it is to have stability in this life. She wants to be that stability for others. She says you're a great dad to your new wife's children and you went to all their graduations.

I have met so many of your sons and daughters. Each of them has the resiliency of a true warrior because they are warriors. Every day and night, they maneuver through predators, hunger, hopelessness, alleys, streets, parks and abandoned buildings. They maneuver through stigmas, judgments and labels placed upon them by people who could not survive a day in their lives. They have been through so much, yet emerge day by day, night by night, a little closer to their own hearts, holding on to their divine vision, mission, dreams and purpose. They are so quick to share and help others in need. Despite the broken hearts, broken dreams and broken glass they've walked through, they're putting the pieces back together, walking back to their beautiful, courageous hearts and remembering they are sacred blessings, miracles and gifts.

Hurricane Harvey and Other Storms

Serving as a Street Outreach Worker before, during, and after Hurricane Harvey may have been one of the most challenging weeks of my life. It took its toll mentally, physically, spiritually and emotionally. Nevertheless, as always, the Creator guided us through the storms. The Creator had me caring for my own family, responding to crisis calls, running supplies to and from organizations, and making sure the youth and our team at our emergency youth shelter were safe.

On the second day of the hurricane, I received a call from a young woman who had been struggling to leave a pimp for a few years. She told me she used the hurricane to get free, hitch a ride for a while, and then walk through waist-deep water to an apartment complex. She gave me the address of where she was, and I was set to go get her and transport her to a shelter. I called some of my friends in law enforcement who told me where the young lady was at was impassable by car, and I would have to walk several miles through waist-high water to reach her. That was fine with me. I got everything I needed together, mapped out the best way to get near the apartment complex where the young lady was, and began to drive past the signs on I-45 south warning drivers the roads a few miles ahead were impassable. The young lady called me while I was driving. She told me she changed her mind, called the pimp, he came and got her, she is safe, and I have nothing to worry about. I was furious. Not at her because that is the cycle. Pimps, who are nothing more than predators, use drugs and many other manipulative and violent tactics to keep their victims on a leash of control through trauma bonding. I was sad for her, furious about the predator that hurts her, and angry the roads were not clear due to the hurricane, because if they were, I would have been able to make it to the young woman before she changed her mind. At least that's what I thought, because no one can really know what would have happened. Speculation is sometimes self-torture. All I know for sure is I was ready, willing and on my way, and for a moment, she was, too. When a Street Outreach Worker responds to a call, and the conclusion is anything less than miraculous, the Street Outreach Worker must go back to the truth that we are planting sacred seeds. There are always miraculous truths beyond the facts, even when what we want to happen for someone is not what happens at that moment.

After Hurricane Harvey passed, even though it left a wake of devastation, it also awoke countless hearts of service. There were people who came to this part of Texas from all over Texas, the United States and the World. I met so many people. Some were in groups. Some were married couples. Some were alone. But they were all searching for the same thing - to serve others. For a few days I saw Street Outreach Workers everywhere. The devastation of Hurricane Harvey was horrific, yet the humanity that arose from thousands, perhaps tens of thousands of human beings was beautiful. I could write for the rest of my life and never be able to share all the lessons the calling of a Street Outreach Worker brings. At one point during Hurricane Harvey, it did not matter if you had money, because even if you did, there was no bread, water or gas to purchase. At the intersection of devastation, danger and loss on a scale as big as Hurricane Harvey, there were those taking advantage of the situation by looting and selling twelve packs of water for fifty dollars. At the same intersection, there were those who went out to serve others in love. In my experience, I have found what James Allen reminded us about is true, *situations do not make a person, situations reveal a person*, or at least what a person has chosen to cultivate.

There were many lessons Hurricane Harvey taught us. One of the many lessons learned during and after Hurricane

Harvey is a strong economy has nothing to do with money, but everything to do with love, faith, hope and charity. When storms such as Hurricane Harvey hit, the veil drops, revealing what is and isn't important, ushering us back to our humanity, as countless people open the most important shelter there is – our hearts. Doesn't our reaction to crises such as Hurricane Harvey reveal that our natural and supernatural instinct is humaneness? Can we cultivate this instinct of humaneness to be lived as a guiding principle of love and service on a daily basis for one another? Can we open our hearts together and take refuge within the Creator through one another in love, prayer, laughter and tears? Street Outreach Workers have answered these questions with a resounding *yes*!

Heaven on Earth May Come in Pieces

As I write this part of the book, it happened again. Sometimes at night images flood my mind and my heart fills with grief. All I have shared in this book and the countless experiences I've chosen not to share in this book, I've never written before, not even in my journal. I have omitted many details in this book regarding the tragedies and abuse I've witnessed for two reasons: to protect the confidentiality of those we serve, and to protect you, the reader, from secondary trauma. I always thought if I touched pen to paper, and truly processed all the abuse, hurt, pain and trauma I've witnessed, I would break. That my heart would literally shatter. I don't think anyone is strong enough to do this work. I don't think anyone is spiritual enough to process this work alone. The good thing is we are never alone. Knowing we are not alone is one thing. Feeling like we are not alone is something else.

What does a Street Outreach Worker do when they return home from back-to-back calls involving kids who've attempted suicide, who've been abused in every way conceivable and inconceivable, with a mixture of tears and blood from families still on your shirt, as the echoes of glass breaking, screams, sirens, or the last words a child said to you play and replay in your mind? I cannot answer those questions for anyone other than myself. Vicarious trauma doesn't just come with fight-or-flight, it also comes with freeze. Frozen moments in time, where looping thoughts replay repeatedly, and no matter how hard you pray and beg the Creator to make it stop, it just doesn't, at least until it runs its course. For me, that's what I must do. I have to allow it to run its course. The course can be directed if we are willing to work with the Creator when those moments come. I would be lying to you if I wrote I didn't have moments when I contemplated suicide. After coming home from some interventions, I contemplated it deeply, not because I wanted to die, but because I wanted the pain to stop. I wanted the looping thoughts to stop. So how do we break the loop of looping thoughts? The best way for me to explain how the Creator and I do it, is by sharing with you an experience I had while working on a ranch many years ago.

I worked on a ranch for a time and we irrigate by hand. That job was the most difficult physical labor I've ever done. In Texas. South Texas. In the summer! We would flood the grapefruit orchard and use shovels to create a barrier of earth around individual grapefruit trees, keeping the water inside to feed the individual tree. Then after a time, we would break the barrier on one side to steer the water to the next tree, and create another barrier, allowing the water to feed that tree. We did this by hand, day and night, living, sleeping and eating out of a truck with no air conditioning for four to five days straight. In the same manner, when traumatic, looping thoughts, which seemingly come out of nowhere, begin to play in my mind, I speak with a trusted friend. That doesn't always take the flood of looping thoughts away, but it breaks the barrier, and with love, directs them in a manner to be of healing and service, not destruction. Street Outreach Workers don't just take horrific events, offer them to the sacred, and allow them to be transformed into healing medicines for a living, but to live. There is no way to have any longevity in the arena of street outreach unless you allow the Creator to break looping thoughts of trauma, so the flow can go in the direction of healing for ourselves and those we serve.

After facilitating a gang prevention and intervention training, one of the participants came up to me and asked, "How do you stay strong?" I knew his question had less to do with his curiosity about me, and more to do with him needing insights for himself.

"By not being afraid to break. That's how I stay strong." He smiled, gave me a hug, and we bestowed the Creator's blessing upon one another before we parted ways.

If we're not afraid to break we can remain strong. In the work of facilitating healing in the lives of abused, exploited and trafficked children, anyone who says they've never been broken is lying, mostly to themselves. This calling will break you, sometimes on a daily and nightly basis. It's what we do with the pieces that matters. It's the beauty that's created from the brokenness that counts. It's the willingness to get up every day and follow the vision to completion. If we are indeed going to see Heaven on Earth, it may just come in pieces. The pieces of humanity's broken hearts, blending together when we stop being afraid to break, and find the courage to share and care for each other's brokenness to build a humanity that is once again humane.

Throughout our lives we encounter many doors masquerading as many things, but the truth is, there are only two doors we have to choose from in every situation - love or fear. When we open the door of fear, our hearts close. When we open the door of love, our hearts open. In the world we live in, there is no act more courageous than living with an open heart. When our hearts are open, love, the most powerful force in the universe, is free to flow through us. Those courageous enough to answer love's call by taking the sacred, seventeen-inch walk from the head back to the heart, allowing love to take them wherever she will, are real warriors, because real warriors love.

Real Warriors Love

Real Warriors Love

Initially, I was going to write this chapter about leadership. As I contemplated all the leaders of the past and present who've made the greatest contributions to this world, the word *leader* does not suffice when describing them. There are many people, past and present, well-known or known only by those in their community, who lived or are currently living a life of love and service. People who selflessly give love and hope despite being attacked, rejected, disrespected, and sometimes, killed. What is considered to be leadership, at least by mainstream standards, pales in comparison when real warriors emerge from the rubble of hate thrown at them and rise in love. Rising with love, real warriors rise *in* power, not *to* it. In love they rise, not to control or sell us anything, but to remind us who we are. They see us as sacred blessings, miracles and gifts. They remind us we're forgiven, worthy, priceless and beautiful. Beyond the field of leaders, they stand on sacred ground as real warriors who have agreed with the Creator about who and what they are, so not even death can detour them from living their sacred visions. They call out to each one of us, reminding us no matter what our titles or professions are, we are all called to be real warriors who love. Perhaps the calling of being a real warrior is something you've ignored or walked away from, but the time has come for you to return to your calling.

Real warriors love because love is what makes a warrior real. Anyone who does anything in love for the benefit of others is a real warrior. The Creator awakens a real warrior in love to awaken love in others. When love is awakened, a vision, no matter how dim it once was, begins to flicker again. First in the hearts and then in the eyes of those who real warriors serve, no matter how severe the trauma they have experienced or are currently experiencing.

For those who may be more religious-based than relationship-based and want to speak about hell and damnation, the youth and young adults I have the privilege to serve have already walked through hell and need not one more moment of condemnation, guilt or blame. They need to experience the sacred, and they will only experience the sacred to the extent love is shared with them. Anyone who fights for anything from their ego will eventually tire and give up. Real warriors get tired and feel frustration, but they never give up. Real warriors keep going through moments of disappointment, heartbreak and setbacks because love carries them through. Love honors the individual's experience. Love cherishes the individual's heart, mind and thought process. It is love, not time, that heals all wounds. Real warriors understand no one is ever *scared straight*. However, real warriors know countless youth, young adults and families who have been loved to healing and positive transformation.

A common phrase in the realm of human services is *meet others where they're at*. Like many sayings and clichés that are true, there is profound wisdom found, not in repeating such phrases, but in living such phrases. Love guides real warriors to know the depths of powerful phrases, not just know *about* powerful phrases. A powerful phrase cracked open by a real warrior's willingness to live it, then deliver it to others in love, provides a powerful transformational experience that may not immediately solve all the challenges someone is experiencing, but will help them place their feet firmly upon a healing road they would have otherwise never considered.

Real Warriors Have Sailed Upon Many Ships

I set sail upon many ships in my life. Some ships I was placed upon as a child, having no choice in the matter. Ships of displacement and growing up in a home with addiction. Ships of understanding, at too early of an age, what most drugs are and how they're used. Ships of my biological father passing on when I was two years old, then being separated from many of my biological family members. Ships of living in several different states and numerous cities before the age of eight years old. Ships of having three different last names before the age of fourteen. Ships of witnessing ambulances and police cars at our home, almost weekly, taking my family members to the hospital because they attempted suicide or overdosed on drugs. Ships of my childhood spent sitting in hospital waiting rooms and chapels, praying, begging God to let my family members live. Ships of momentary stability when my mother remarried a man who became my dad because he provided love, direction and consistency. And right when my dad's love, direction and consistency were beginning to take root and flourish in our lives, he passed on when I was sixteen years old, then once again, my world crumbled before me and beneath me.

There were the ships I willingly walked inside due to trauma. Ships that promised many things. Promises to numb my pain. Promises to help me forget. Promises I belonged. Promises that all my needs would be met. The ships of drug and alcohol abuse, eventually leading to ships of suicide attempts and homelessness. Promises, so many promises, yet all those ships filled with empty promises, every single one of them, crashed violently upon the shore of desperation. As I sat on the shore of desperation in the wreckage of fear, more ships arrived with more promises, and none of them could fill the void in my heart until the most important ship came to my rescue. The invaluable, priceless ship that saved my life and countless other lives is revealed in a short story I wrote, *A Tale of Six Ships.*

A Tale of Six Ships

Upon the shore of desperation, many seagoing vessels, all large ships with countless passengers came to me. The captains of each ship claimed to be able to take me across the tumultuous waters of uncertainty and deliver me safely to my mission, vision, dreams and purpose. I listened closely to the captains of each ship tell me all they have to offer.

The first captain to plead her case to me was the captain of the *Leader* ship. The captain of the *Leader* ship was strong, assertive and bold in reminding me that for me to reach my destiny I must board her ship. She cited my inabilities to lead and inspire and guaranteed her ship held the answers. The passengers upon the *Leader* ship didn't add anything to the discourse, only regurgitation of what the captain repeatedly said. The captain told me if I wanted to become the person I am supposed to be, I needed to enter her ship and experience leadership.

After the captain of the *Leader* ship concluded her plea, the captain of the *Citizen* ship spoke. He pointed out I needed to be part of something bigger than myself, like him and his ship. When he made that observation aloud, all the passengers waved their flags of the *Citizen* ship and cheered. The captain told me that for me to experience life correctly all I had to do was enter his ship and experience citizenship.

Next, I heard from the captain of the *Hard* ship. She went on and on, telling me about how important it is to struggle. "No pain, no gain," she emphasized repeatedly. I don't remember a lot of what she said, other than the words she used most – struggle, grind and sacrifice. All the passengers in the *Hard* ship had eyes of steel as they periodically yelled caveman-like grunts each time the captain told me about the necessity to struggle, grind, sacrifice and feel pain. The captain told me I would eventually find all I am searching for if I entered her ship and experienced hardship.

The captain of the *Owner* ship stood and began to point out all I didn't have that I could truly call my own. All the passengers were quiet, seemingly in their own little worlds. None of them were interacting with one another. The captain didn't focus on my loneliness and isolation from people, but on my lack of owning things, and assured me I would feel whole if I entered his ship and experienced ownership.

After listening to the captains and some of the passengers from the ships of *Leader*, *Citizen*, *Hard* and *Owner* explain why I needed to travel with them, I began to cry from frustration and sadness. As I cried, I heard voices from the *Leader* ship say, "Come with us and you won't be sad any longer because we have your answers." Then I heard voices from the *Citizen* ship bellow, "Travel with us and you'll belong." Voices from the *Hard* ship shouted, "See? You need to toughen up. Join us and you'll be strong." Yells from the *Owner* ship implored, "Let's go buy things so you can be somebody."

As they all yelled at me, although my spirit knew there was something more, much more, beyond what any of them were offering, my mind began to grow weary. When our minds grow weary, if we're already alone and in quiet desperation, sometimes we entertain offers of mediocrity. Perhaps not everyone, but at that moment, I did. In that crucial moment where I felt the only choices I had were in front of me, seemingly out of nowhere, another ship arrived. And when it did, the ships of *Leader, Citizen, Hard* and *Owner* fell silent and departed from the shore. The ship that arrived was different because when it came upon the shore of desperation to meet me, no one on the ship said a word, and as far as I could tell, there was no captain.

All the people exited the ship, walked upon the shore of desperation and surrounded me. They let me cry. They hugged me. And they allowed me to express myself without interruption or interpretation. After I was done crying and my genuine smile came back to me, as it always will after tears of purification cleanse us, I asked, "Who's the captain?"

A woman with glistening eyes pointed upwards, "We all have the same Captain, my dear. That's Who sent us to you."

Mystified, I questioned, "What's the name of your ship?"

An elderly man with a cane limped towards me smiling, as the woman with glistening eyes and the others began to dismantle their ship and use the pieces to light a fire while singing the most beautiful songs I've ever heard. The elderly man wiped away the remnants of my tears still streaming down my cheeks, then gently held my hands as he shared, "Our ship is the *Friend* ship. We're not here to lead you anywhere. We're here to be with you. We're not here to tell you what you need to do to belong. We're here to belong with you because you already belong. You've always belonged. We're not here to convince you to struggle, grind or experience pain. There's been too much of that in your life and in the world already. We're not here to buy, sell or barter, because what we offer is what you already have, which is everything. You just need to remember you never had to become somebody or something, because you're so much more than a *body* or a *thing*. You're a sacred blessing, miracle and gift. Together, in love, prayer, laughter and tears, we'll light a fire and keep it burning bright, eat beautiful foods and sing songs of joy and beauty. We'll take care of one another with only the Creator as our Captain. You don't have to go anywhere. We're here with you, using the light from the fire the *Friend* ship provides to keep us warm. Eradicating darkness and transforming this shore of desperation into a ship that never has to set sail because it will always meet us

172

where we're at, wherever we are, when we need it most –
relationship."

Real Warriors Love Principles for Living

There have been countless real warriors the Creator has sent
to me upon my shore of desperation throughout my life.
Some were biological family, some were friends, and others
were strangers who've become my chosen family. Crossing
tumultuous waters, they went out of their way to find me and
remind me who I am. It is they who ignited a fire of love and
service in my life. Through their unwavering love, despite my
continual protests I was nothing and no one, worthy of only
torment and despair, they fed me, housed me, clothed me,
purified me, guided me, and reminded me I am here with a
great purpose given to me by the Great One Who created
me. There is no way for me to thank them, other than
extending the love they gave me to you.

Whatever you pour your life into will pour life into you.
Whether you've written a book, cultivated a healthy
relationship, earned a degree or diploma, became an amazing
parent or grandparent, started a business, created music, or
overcame more things than anyone will ever know so that
just choosing to be alive today is a victory, celebrate your
victories! Celebrate your progress. Honor them. Be grateful
for them. Be grateful for you. I am grateful for you.

Following your vision, mission, dreams and purpose has little to do with a final product or reaching a finish line. It's about the process. It's about what the voyage cultivates within you. It's about the path bringing you back to the truth of who you are in the Creator, within the sacred, and within your own beautiful heart. The journey, however you choose to walk it, is the sacred seventeen-inch walk from your head back to your heart.

There are seventeen real warriors love principles for living I will share with you. These principles for living have come from the Creator, birthed through me during some excruciating moments. They've sprung forth from moments of desperation where I thought there was no hope, no point and no future. They've carried myself and thousands of youth and young adults I've been blessed to serve across the dangerous waters of despair and hopelessness. They are a sacred scroll that survived the shore of desperation and were uncovered beneath the wreckage of fear with the light of love and relationship. They are principles for living, and if you choose to live them, they will walk you back to your own heart. They will guide you in reclaiming your sacred vision, mission, dreams and purpose. Most importantly, they will guide you and equip you to deliver the light of love and relationship to others who are standing upon a shore of desperation.

Originally, I was going to explain how each principle came to be, the crucial moments in my life when each of them arrived, and how the Creator has guided me in using them to serve others. Perhaps in another book or when we meet face-to-face. For now, like the *Friend* ship that arrived on the shore of desperation, I will just share the principles with you so each one of them exits the *Friend* ship and meets you where you are. Allow them to light a fire of love and relationship within you. Contemplate them in prayer and meditation. Each one of them will mean something different to you at different times throughout your life. I love you. Thank you for taking this journey with me. You are a sacred blessing, miracle and gift.

Real Warriors Love Principles for Living

1. Find that which fills you when you give it away, because that's your calling.
2. Follow your calling. Where it takes you to is uncertain. Where it takes you from is the certain suffering of not following it.
3. Work for purpose, not money. If the only opportunities you see are the ones that include a paycheck, you're missing out on many blessed moments of love, service and spiritual growth.

4. During the challenging times, remember that it is a moment in your life, not the rest of your life.

5. Be compassionate with yourself and others. If you don't have time to be compassionate, you've forgotten what time is for.

6. You are a sacred blessing, miracle and gift. You'll never experience what you are while practicing what you are not.

7. Don't deny the light you prayed for just because you don't like the lamp that was chosen to bring it.

8. If you want to help others with their spiritual growth, work on your own. If you want to work on your spiritual growth, help others.

9. If you're never wrong, there will be many things you'll never make right.

10. Don't deny your miracles. Your miracles will often appear when you feel unworthy of them for three reasons: To remind you that you are worthy of miracles. To show you that you are a miracle. To move through you to bless others with miracles.

11. Let your works be an offering to the Sacred, and the Sacred will offer you *Its* works.

12. Count your scars as the number of times you've been healed, not wounded.

13. Forgive the unforgiveable.

14. For as long as your life is someone else's fault, it's not your life.

15. Don't allow the memories you didn't get to have, stop you from making the memories you deserve.

16. Intergenerational healing is more powerful than intergenerational trauma.

17. Do the math – God's math.

God's Math

I'm not a theologian nor a mathematician
We know God through love, not religion
Love given is only addition
In God's math there exists no division

Acknowledgements

First and foremost, I thank You, God, my savior Jesus Christ and the Holy Spirit. I love You. Thank You.

My loving wife and children, you are all gracious, kind, compassionate and beautiful. I want you to know it is because of God and each one of you that I am growing into the best version of myself. Thank you for helping me grow. Thank you for being my greatest teachers and inspiration. I love you

Thank you to all of my ancestors for your contributions, prayers and sacrifices that make it possible for me to follow what the Creator has assigned me to do.

Uncle Clare and Aunt Patty, your example of strength, consistency, love and leadership has influenced countless people, but for me, your loving example has shaped and saved my life. Thank you. I love you.

Thank you, Dick Skoglund and the entire Ramchargers race team who supported me and my mother immensely after my dad, Phil Goulet, passed on in 1988.

His Holiness The 14th Dalai Lama, thank you for taking the time to write a beautiful foreword for this book. Your life is a testament to the power of love and compassion that you teach by both words and example.

My brother, Mike Kermon, you've given more than most in love and service to others on the streets every night for many years. Thank you for being an inspiration and an example of how to be.

Sam Roman, thank you for being my friend, brother and the best Street Outreach Worker I've ever been blessed to serve with.

Kim Wensaut, even with all the things you were juggling, you took the time to organize and edit my writing, experiences and ideas to help manifest this book. You are an amazing sister, writer, poet, editor, warrior and human being.

Thank you, Lavack family. You took me in when I had nowhere to go. You kept me safe, fed me, guided me, and loved me through a difficult time. You not only treated me as family, you took me in and became my family. I love you.

Uncle Les and aunt Kat, thank you for your love, counsel, acceptance, and leading me back to God.

Richard Ramos and D.J. Vanas, no matter how busy the two of you are, you both have always supported my work. More important than supporting my work, you've always made yourselves available to pray for me, encourage me and guide me. You are both dear to me. You are both warriors for the Creator and all that is good. It is my honor to know both of you.

Thank you, Tara Pretends Eagle Weber. Your continued love and support over the years has been so important for me and my family. Most importantly, thank you for your decades of loving, ferocious advocacy for the missing, murdered and marginalized.

Jayla The Self Esteem Queen, thank you for being a living example of love, service and leadership. Your life is a testimony to the power of God's love.

Erica Manuel, thank you for believing in and trusting what God has called me to do. Your love, support, prayers and encouragement are divine blessings for me and my family.

Akello Stone, thank you for living a life of love, service & leadership. You are an amazing youth mentor, professor, actor, thinker, writer and human being. Thank you for being a bright light in this world.

Lesa Day, you are a prayer warrior. Thank you for always supporting my family and I in love, prayer and counsel. God bless you.

To some of the trailblazers of youth programs and community development I've been blessed to know, I'd like to thank Lucy Harrison, Dr. Lynette Findley, Angela Reyes, Andrea White, Mike Vazquez, Deanna Francis, Thurman Bear and Juan Patiño.

Tome and Nancy Roubideaux, your love, time and guidance has greatly enriched my life and the lives of those I am blessed to serve. Thank you for being an amazing uncle and auntie to me. I love you both.

Joseph Brave-Heart, ciye (elder brother), thank you for your loving guidance, patience, time, teachings and excellent sense of humor.

Kelly Kiyoshk, your love, service and leadership brings healing to countless people throughout many communities. Thank you for choosing love's path. You are a real warrior.

Thank you, John Bracken, for all your years of love, service and leadership that I've been blessed to learn and grow from. Thank you for being a true servant leader.

Thank you to all my coworkers at Bridgeway Emergency Youth Shelter and the entire Yes to Youth organization. You are enriching and saving lives every day and every night.

Jamie Parker and Marcel Lue, thank you for being amazing directors of Bridgeway Emergency Youth Shelter. Both the staff and the youth we serve are blessed by your leadership.

To all the Street Outreach Workers of past, present and future, our calling is great. May your love be strong, your honor pure, your light bright – thank you for living a life of love and service.

I want to thank the Gandy, Montelongo, Bauknecht, Roman, McCullough and Trusty families for your care, love and support throughout many seasons, but especially during the seasons when the only thing I had to offer were my tears. Thank you. I love you.

About the Author

In his twenty-seven-year career in youth development, Anthony Goulet has led gang prevention and intervention programs, prisoner reentry programs, and worked as a Certified Addictions Counselor with gang affiliated youth and adults providing relapse prevention for substance abuse and criminal behavior. Anthony continues to work full-time as a Street Outreach Crisis Counselor who serves homeless, runaway, exploited, and sex trafficked youth and young adults by facilitating interventions, rescues, and safe transports on the streets; he also provides longer term services of counseling and family reunification within an emergency youth shelter. Due to his personal testimony, twenty-seven years of professional experience, and the ability to articulate the process of transformation with passion and beautiful storytelling, Anthony continues to be sought by organizations as a transformational speaker, trainer and consultant.

Other Books by Anthony Goulet

God, Help Me Tie My Shoes!
The Sacred Contract of Fatherhood

The Four

Rain of Thoughts

www.anthonygoulet.com

67203522R00114

Made in the USA
Columbia, SC
24 July 2019